Socialism Explained

In June 1983 the Labour Party, under the leadership of Michael Foot, suffered one of the heaviest electoral defeats in its history. A new leader emerged and the Party resolved to avoid failure on such a large scale in the future.

Socialism Explained is a lively and up-to-date book which analyses the socialist movement in Britain and the other countries of the world and concludes that socialism is *bound to fail* and that, in the words of the *New Statesman*, 'After a hundred years, it is time for Labour to bury Marx'. In Part 1 Arthur Seldon describes how socialism has held out promises of the good life for people of all ages and occupations, but usually it has resulted in lower living standards and, in some parts of the world, loss of liberty. Socialism in the 1980s is no more than larger doses of regulations, controls, centralisation of political power and bureaucracy—only the slogans are new. All the major problems that remain to be solved by mankind—poverty, inequality, unemployment, inflation, accountability, freedom and monopoly—are best dealt with by an open society with free markets. After a hundred years of broken promises and false hopes, Arthur Seldon explains why it is time for the millions who looked to socialists as their natural champions to bury socialism and take on the task faced by non-socialist political parties of creating prosperity *without* destroying liberty.

Brian Crozier's first example in Part 2 is, naturally, the Soviet Union. Lenin's 'first workers' state' and home of the longest continuous experiment in socialist economics. Excluding the *Communist* aspects (purges, massacres, repression), he finds a permanent lack of ability to emulate the achievements of 'capitalism', a huge war economy and a heavy dependence on Western technology and money. He goes on to analyse socialism in all its varieties in Eastern Europe, including the Yugoslav experiment and Romanian Stalinism, and quotes a telling speech by Fidel Castro in Cuba, where the Soviets pick up the bills. His Third World examples are India, Burma (the 'cult of scarcity') and Tanzania (the horrors of collectivisation). In his last chapter he weighs the cost of welfare socialism in the United States, Sweden, France and West Germany, then looks at the Austrian experiment: successful, but *not* socialism.

Brilliantly illustrated by Michael Cummings, *Socialism Explained* has an underlying seriousness in its approach to the failure of socialism over the last hundred years and in its presentation of the political and economic problems that we all face in the future.

Socialism Explained

Brian Crozier and Arthur Seldon
With cartoons by Cummings

THE SHERWOOD PRESS

First published 1984

© Brian Crozier and Arthur Seldon 1984

The Sherwood Press Ltd, 88 Tylney Road, London E7 OLY

ISBN 0 907671 06 3

Set in Times by BookEns, Saffron Walden, Essex
Printed and bound by The Burlington Press, Foxton, Cambridge

Contents

Preface *by Brian Crozier*   vii

PART ONE *by Arthur Seldon*

PROMISES, PROMISES

   Prologue: the Socialist God that Failed   3
1 Socialism: Heaven or Hell?   5
2 Socialism at Last—Official   12
3 The Socialist Guilty Secret   22
4 The Sad Saga of Incorrigible Socialism   29
5 After a Hundred Years: Time to Bury Socialism   49
   Envoi   63

PART TWO *by Brian Crozier*

EVERYWHERE A FAILURE

   Prologue: the Universal Rules of Socialism   67
6 The Soviet Prototype   72
7 Socialism in Eastern Europe   82
8 Far Eastern Models—and Cuba   94
9 Third World Socialism   104
10 Welfare Socialism   114
   Index   131

Preface

by Brian Crozier

It was natural for the disillusioned young to turn to socialism in the 1930s. And, let us face it, there was plenty to be disillusioned about. Although Australians by birth, our family had settled in London in 1930. As a family, we were badly hit by the Great Depression, with the main breadwinner unemployed and a teen-aged elder brother and sister to provide an income of sorts from temporary jobs.

'Capitalism' seemed to have broken down, as Karl Marx had said it would. The distant Soviet Union, largely unknown apart from official propaganda and the effusive reporting of George Bernard Shaw, the Webbs and other fellow-travellers, seemed to provide a socialist answer. In 1937, I joined Victor Gollancz's Left Book Club, and swallowed almost whole one of its first offerings, the monumental nonsense of Sidney and Beatrice Webb's *Soviet Communism: A New Civilisation* (the first edition of which carried a question-mark, removed for the one that reached Left Book Club readers).

Well, all this is a long time ago. I voted enthusiastically for Labour in 1945, but left British austerity behind to return to my native country with my own family in 1948 only to find that a Labour government had come to power there too. By 1950, I was pretty disillusioned with socialism. But not yet fully cured. It was not until about 1960 that the sensational performance of West Germany's 'economic miracle' and the writings of the French economist, Professor Maurice Allais, convinced me of the infinite superiority of 'capitalism' (the market economy, free enterprise and some form of political democracy) over socialism in all its forms.

Today, when the failure of socialism everywhere is patent, it does seem a pity that so many young people should still fall victims to its supposed enchantments. One reason undoubtedly is that despite the surge of the 'radical right' in recent years, the proportion of published texts denigrating capitalism and singing the praises of Marxism and other forms of socialism is still overwhelming in all our Western countries.

I was happy, therefore, to join Arthur Seldon in this modest attempt to redress the balance. My excuse is that 'I have been there' and it just doesn't work.

PART ONE

Promises, Promises
Arthur Seldon

Prologue: The Socialist God that Failed

The Socialist god has long since lost its ability to fire the minds of men.
Professor J. M. Buchanan (1982)

In the century since the death of Karl Marx in 1883 socialism has held out promises of the good life to erudite scholars in all subjects, to recipient students, hopeful young people in general, and not least the trusting working masses.

After a hundred years in which socialism has been applied in varying forms in all the continents of the world, it has failed to keep its promises. What good it has claimed to have done for a time in some countries where the people had been subjugated has cost them their liberty, living standards, not least often life itself — in Eastern Europe (including the USSR) in numbers that exceed the carnage of Nazism.

The consequences of socialism follow wherever and however it is practised, not least in the socialist ('public sector') parts of otherwise liberal capitalist states—in Britain in the nationalised industries, public corporations, state education, the National Health Service, council housing, and local government. In societies with democratic cultures, in West Europe, North America and Australasia, the more savage consequences have been held at bay. But the effects on liberty, equity, harmony, efficiency and living standards have been reproduced in essence: the difference is in degree. Yet socialism is still taught in Britain by politicians, academics, writers, playwrights, and by clerics who exploit their spiritual influence to urge economic policies some of them do not seem to understand.

Socialism continues to beguile the young, excite the scholar, bewitch the priest, entice the poor with promises of prosperity and liberty. And if the sceptics point to its evils wherever it is practised, ardent defendants claim that the 'socialism' we have known round the world is not socialism: 'real' socialism has not yet been tried.

A hundred years is time enough to call the bluff of socialism. Whatever good it might yet do in so far unknown forms, the slight chance of doubtful socialist success entails the huge cost of the opportunity lost to perfect the only other system that has demonstrated round the world in the East as well as the West, its capacity to raise living standards *without* destroying liberty. The market economy has been given a bad name by its detractors, but a good name by its record in the real world. A second century of preaching, teaching, promising, organising for a socialism that shows no signs of doing better than it did in the first is too high a price to pay for losing the hope of spreading higher living standards *with* liberty in all the continents of the world, developed and developing, South and North: not least in the poor socialist countries of Eastern Europe, Asia and Africa, where promises still outrun performance.

A recent writer in the *New Statesman* said 'After a hundred years, it's time for Labour to bury Marx'. My conclusion for newcomers, seduced as millions have been by the promises of socialism, is 'After a hundred years it's time to bury *socialism*. The workers of the world have been deceived long enough.'

1

Socialism: Heaven or Hell?

Socialism straddles the range of the human spirit—from the saintly to the venal. It is urged by good men—like the Methodist cleric Lord Soper—as a Christian society of mutual brotherhood and love, compassion and sharing. And it is exploited by selfish people hungry for power to rule over their fellow-men.

The socialist contradiction is insoluble. Many who advocate socialism see it as a heaven. More who suffer from it see it as a hell.

Socialism cannot be judged by the good intentions of its saints. It must be judged by the result of its practitioners.

The forms taken by socialism vary widely, from the relatively mild in Austria and Sweden to the severe in the USSR. To judge any given form at any time in any country is to be met by the objection of socialists that it is not socialism as they see it, or as it could be. At the extremes there are socialists who deny there is or has been any socialism in the world anywhere. So it cannot be judged at all. Socialism cannot be condemned because it does not exist—yet. Or if they concede there are elements of socialism in one country or another—the USSR is the most difficult to deny—it is too soon to judge; it should be given more time. They will claim, eloquently, that socialism must be given more time till the end of time to show that it can achieve its objectives.

For this short joint book with Brian Crozier I shall state the main features of what, over fifty years of study and thought, I have understood by 'socialism', and discuss its effects and consequences (Crozier will analyse socialism in various countries). If readers do not agree with my statement of the essence of socialism, they should read no further. They have retired from the argument. With other socialists, even though they may not wholly agree with my understanding of 'socialism', a dialogue or debate can help both sides to remove ambiguities but it will help mainly

5

the newcomer—young or old—by clarifying what he or she can or cannot expect from socialism.

Socialism in principle, in ideal conception, is the economic system in which the (main) means of production (human and material resources) are controlled or operated not privately (by individuals, partners, firms, co-operatives, mutual groups) in the light of their reading of what the people in general, in their given state of knowledge, would like the resources to produce, but by a relatively small number of elected or self-selected people with 'public' authority, access to information, expert advice and power to direct the allocation of the resources to the occupations, industries and regions where they judge they will most productively respond to the wants, demands, wishes, preferences, 'needs' of the people. This is the most benign definition of the socialist goal I can formulate. In the real world socialism is more venal, in some countries tyrannical. The human face is taught by socialists; the ugly face appears only after it is created. And then it is too late.

The question then, is which of two systems—decentralised privately decided production (broadly described technically as a market economy, generally as private enterprise, or historically (and hysterically by socialists) as 'capitalism') or centralised 'publicly' controlled socialist production—is the more likely to serve the people better.

This is the essence of the argument. There are many variations of socialism. After the 1979 and 1983 rejections by the electors, socialists are again anxiously, candidly and disingenuously debating among themselves* which road to socialism is left to them. The gradual, parliamentary path of democratic socialism or social democracy (although I shall deny that democracy is compatible with socialism)? The insurrectionary path of revolution taken in October 1917 in Russia? The new 'third way', which Marxist socialists confusedly conceive as a half-way house between fighting and non-fighting (voting, persuasion, electing assemblies of representatives)? Or the fourth way of a new hybrid Eurocommunism which works with bourgeois government (as in Italy) or inside it (as in France)—in a new or last desperate approach to use government—any government—as the creator of work or producer of services for all?

Whatever the paths to socialism, envisaged (or conjured) by the visionaries, the essence of its political and economic system is that socialism works by 'representation'. In theory, everyone is 'represented'

---

* As they did in *Marxism Today* (March 1983), between Professor Hobsbawm, Bob Rowthorne, Professor Ralph Miliband and Anne Sassoon.

on local committees, regional soviets, national councils. The elected bodies—runs socialist doctrine—work for the equal good of the whole people. Their sole purpose is to serve it. The question is how far they should 'democratically' respond to its expressed wishes (assuming they can be discovered, assembled and transmitted in time to the requisite authorities and redistributed to the myriads of production units) or provide the services their 'representatives' paternalistically consider are for the general good of the people. In short, how far do the people elect the representatives to do their bidding as their 'agents', and how far do the 'representatives', once elected, make the decisions for the people?

This is the glory of socialism—on paper. This is the vision that has produced the eloquence and the perorations of the Michael Foots and Neil Kinnocks of British socialism. To them, it remains an *inspiration, a goal, a vision*. It must never descend to earth to become a piece of economic/political machinery working day by day that can be examined—both by enthusiasts and by sceptics—as it works and judged on its merits in fulfilling its ambitious promises. It is always a splendid exciting star in the sky. That is why Foot was angered by the Social Democrat David Owen for removing the word 'socialism' from the second edition of his political testament, *Face the Future*, and perhaps even more with the Social Democrat Michael (Lord) Young, for appropriating the name of Tawney for the Social Democratic 'think tank'.* But Foot rose to his majestic eloquence in reprimanding the two Labour renegades in *The Times* (1 February 1982):

> Some of us can recall how proudly and passionately he [Tawney] pronounced the word socialism, and scorned those who would not understand its *true origin, meaning and glory*. (*My italics*.)

For visionary socialists self-evidently socialism will always remain a state of society with desirable objectives—liberty, equality, comradeship, compassion—yet to be reached, not a state of affairs that has arrived in the real world, in some form, somewhere, to be judged as it is with all its 'glorious' warts. All known efforts to achieve socialism are, for many socialists, poor shadows of the 'glorious' substance. For them, there is *now* no socialism *in their* image anywhere in the world. All the known efforts have gone wrong, fallen by the way, made tragic mistakes,

* To my surprise, *The Guardian* (31 May 1982) allowed me an article to explain why Tawney was not a good choice.

failed to understand the purpose, fallen into unfortunately wrong hands—*they are no test of 'glorious' socialism.*

Michael Foot maintained this pretence with verbal agility until he was asked, by what he may have thought a friendly newspaper thousands of miles from Westminster, what was the nearest that could be found to what he saw as socialism. He was caught off his guard. His reply—'war-time Britain'—would have been given by many socialists, but it would be repudiated by nine-tenths of the remaining 8 million Labour voters in the 1980s if he had explained to them precisely what lives it would re-create for them now, as it created for their parents and grand-parents for five years from 1939 to 1945. I discuss this glorious socialism—the only form recognised by many socialists like the older man who in 1983 wanted to be, or the younger man who wants to be, socialist Prime Minister of Britain in 1988—in Chapter 2.

Let socialist intellectuals pursue such ennobling visions. My charge against them is that they have misled the people long enough—not only for a hundred years since the death of Marx in 1883, but before that to the early French socialists—Babeuf (1760–97), who demanded 'public ownership', and the Comte de Saint-Simon (1760–1825), who called for central planning, and long before that to the Utopians, millennarians, Nirvanarians, and the purveyors of cornucopias in Paradise from the dawn of history.

It is time this deception by promise, a string of South Sea Bubbles, wills-o-the-wisp, pies-in-the-sky, and jam tomorrow, is replaced by examination of the *performance* of socialism in the real world—what it can be expected to achieve, why it has not achieved it, and, I shall argue, why it cannot, why it *must* fail.

Socialists, especially Marxists, make much of the continuing appeal of Marxism that people—especially young students—look to it as an alternative to 'the internal contradictions of capitalism'. If there are such contradictions, it is clear from its record that, *despite* instabilities and its other faults (discussed below), capitalism has surmounted its contradictions and made them secondary to its achievements. My reply to socialists who have long lived on the 'contradictions of capitalism' is that the contradictions of socialism are not only more fundamental but *impossible to eliminate.*

I discuss below also the many defects of socialism, not least the impossibility of running socialism at all unless it uses the 'capitalist' device of market pricing to discover what the people want and therefore where to allocate resources. I point to the incidental but crippling and decisive defects of socialism generally overlooked by socialists. Here I deal with its central, fatal, contradiction: that the *socialist* device of 'representation' *cannot* discover what the people who are represented want their representatives to do. There is no way out of this contradiction of unrepresentative 'representatives' who transform the nominally represented sovereign people into the unrepresented puppets who have to take what socialism produces or lump it: from spam in wartime Britain to food, clothes, homes and much else in peacetime Russia. The only device that creates the pretence that the system is 'working' at all is for the representatives to give the people—the represented—what the *representatives*—the planners, officials and *apparatchiks*—judge they *would* want if it had been possible to discover the information. The contradiction, in short, is that, instead of socialism comprising the satisfied wishes of millions of socialists, the wishes have to fit into the socialist plan. Socialism is the system in which the tiny but powerful tail of socialist representatives—planners, commissars, *apparatchiks*, anyone with political power—wags the large but castrated dog of the socialised people.

It is, of course, technically feasible for countries with large resources of workers, technology and land to produce large *quantities* of goods and services of assorted types, sizes, shapes and qualities. And any centralised body with power to direct people where to work, at what job, for how long, can amass an impressive inventory of acres of food, tons of coal, square yards of cloth, millions of houses and so on. But all this can mean nothing or very little.

The economic problem that faces humanity is not of this kind. It is to produce the array of goods and services from given scarce resources in the shapes, sizes, quantities that the *people* want *without* transforming them into passive recipients of the products of conscript labour. And that has not been done by socialism anywhere in the world. There are socialist countries that can produce long lists of goods and services, but no-one knows how far they are what the people wanted. Socialism is a vast machine for churning out piles of goods marked 'Take it or leave it'. And it adds insult to injury: 'If you don't like it, shut up.' Or in Britain, 'Buy it even if it is inefficient or inferior because it keeps jobs going even if they churn out out-dated, or second-rate goods that can't compete in the world'.

The ineradicable flaw of socialism, as long as it remains real,

orthodox, centralised socialism, is that it has no mechanism for measuring *satisfaction*. It normally measures its performance by *quantities*. Numbers of shoes, boxes of oranges, dozens of stockings, tons of coal, miles of passenger journeys—all of which may tell us very little or nothing unless we also know they are *what the people want* and are prepared to pay for in preference to other products. It is only now, after it was pointed out by 'bourgeois' ('capitalist') economists sixty years ago and more, that socialism—transferring resources from private to 'public' ownership—would solve nothing, and end in chaos, because it had no calculating mechanism for registering values, that socialist economists—even more in Europe than in Britain—are at last beginning to accept generally that there is something vital missing from socialism. In Britain socialists continue to peddle the old dreams, hopes and promises. Individual socialist economists in Europe—even a few in Russia—have patiently and wearily tried to explain, but the excitement with the 'glories' of 'public ownership' has made socialists deaf. The beautiful carriage of 'socialism' was their pride and joy. But it would not move without a horse called the market; and that was too painful to consider. In 1983, a hundred years after Marx, a book by a socialist economist, Professor Alec Nove,* perhaps at last shocked them into reality: he tells them, patiently but relentlessly, that socialism will not work without markets, that is without capitalism! I have to add that the horse he may at last persuade socialists to accept would shake the 'glorious' but creaky state carriage of socialism into smithereeens. For it is an old-fashioned frame, too slow, too clumsy to change and too inflexible for the highly refined computer of the market that produces rapid results and requires rapid information to process.

The Marxist Professor Hobsbawm, who has been teaching history to generations of students at Birkbeck College, told some fellow-Marxists that the task of allocating resources—the horse—will really have to be thought about now that Marxists are considering 'the socialist transformation of Western society'. This intellectual irresponsibility—or perhaps gall—echoes the dismay of Emanuel Shinwell, who had advocated the nationalisation of the mines all his life and, when he found himself Minister of Fuel, discovered he had given no thought to the method of nationalisation.

So, whatever the *claims* that socialism is, or could be, heaven, what is it in the real world? Is it heaven? Or is it hell?

* *The Economics of Feasible Socialism*, Allen and Unwin, 1983.

2

Socialism at Last—Official

Socialists are congenitally reluctant to have the case for socialism judged by examining socialism in practice. They are forever devising new variants of socialism that they claim, or hope, will avoid the defects of other variants. A new effort with a chilling defeatist flavour is *Socialism in a Cold Climate** which yet again repeats, regurgitates and re-cooks the same old recipes for the 1980s—more state coercion.

As a going concern in real everyday life, socialism acknowledged as such by socialists who, as soon as it fails, turn to new formulations for the old fallacies, is about as elusive as the Scarlet Pimpernel.

> We seek it here,
> We seek it there,
> We critics seek it everywhere:
> Is it realism?
> Or is it phantasm?
> That demn'd elusive
> Socialism.

Always, we are told, socialism in this or that country is not socialism as it should be; or could be, or would be if socialists—from Khrushchev to Callaghan—had not made 'mistakes'. So criticisms of it don't count.

After every rejection by the people at general elections, socialists gird their loins to refine their socialism. They are at it again after the June rejection in 1983. Again the promises are re-spun.

At last, a well-known socialist has had the courage, or—because he

---

* Its authors are mostly from the London School of Economics, largely the creation of the naive, *leichtgläubig* Webbs, who foolishly saw *A New Civilisation* in the Russia of the 1930s at the height of Stalin's terror.

does not understand the risks he has run—the foolhardiness, to say where this socialism, or democratic socialism as he prefers, can be found. Michael Foot, whose socialism always rested on emotion and slogan rather than economic understanding, incautiously told the American liberal newspaper, *The Washington Post*, in December 1982 (here, 'liberal' is used in the American sense of semi-socialist, not the classical European sense of liberty-oriented or libertarian):

> The best example I have seen of democratic socialism operating in this country was during the Second World War. Then we ran Britain highly efficiently and got everybody into a job ... It was a democratic society with a common aim.

This notion of a 'common aim' is the common illusion of all fairy-tale romantic socialists down to the new Labour leader with old ideas, Neil Kinnock.

Unintentionally, Mr Foot revealed the mind of the true socialist down the ages until our day, congenitally happiest when organising, controlling, marshalling people who have been relieved of their liberties—for their own good, of course. For all his talk of liberty, the socialist is essentially a sergeant-major, with, of course, a heart of gold. And war is his happy hunting-ground, for the sense of crisis, the state of emergency, the imminence of external danger is the ideal soil for submission to authority—unquestioning, passive, fatalistic. It is then that the managers, the organisers, the regulators, the controllers—the sergeant-majors—can best do their stuff.

That is why socialism is accepted in war, and why war has produced socialism that then lasts into the peace. Russian communism grew out of the First World War. In the Second World War all the main participants tolerated socialism to a smaller or larger extent: National socialism in Germany, fascist socialism in Italy, limited 'democratic' socialism in Britain, even in the USA. That is why socialists are forever creating crises and emergencies by military language: the 'struggle' against capitalism, the 'battle' for equality, the 'rising' against oppressors, the 'revolt' of the masses. Socialism thrives in crisis.

Socialists love to conjure the flavour of apocalyptic excitement, for then the people become malleable. But that is the socialists' fatal mistake, and the people's fatal danger. The socialists' mistake is to say that what worked in war could work in peace. The people's danger is to tolerate wartime economy after the war, for the longer it lasts the more difficult it is to dissolve. The Russians know that, having accepted, or tolerated, socialism for sixty-five years after the First World War, it will require upheaval, a moral, a cultural earthquake, if not bloody armed rebellion, to dislodge. (I nevertheless believe it will happen within twenty years.)

The post-war welfare state was consolidated because of the fatal mistake that what worked in war could work in peace. That was the teaching of sociologists led by the late Richard Titmuss. And we are now stuck with the welfare state, even though it has gone sour, and the small good it does is outweighed by its disproportionate harm.

What, then, was the wartime system that Mr Foot offered the British people? How did it work? What were its results? Would the British really want it back forty years later in the 1980s? Would the socialism of Kinnock, essentially the same, work differently?

First, to ensure 'fair shares' in wartime, unequal ownership of money was replaced by more or less equal distribution of coupons according to 'need': free choice in the shops according to prices was replaced by rationing. For two centuries since the Scottish David Hume, economists had judged that in a siege economy, when supplies could not rapidly respond to changing demands through price, rationing was the next best system of distribution. But it was a necessary evil because it destroyed the price signals to producers, who had to take their orders from wartime siege 'planners'. So distribution was equal and 'fair—but there were shortages, queues and—what the admirers of that siege-time socialism conveniently ignore—under-the-counter deals, favouritism, bribery, blackmail, corruption and a lot of other symptoms of socialism—even in wartime. And not least among them was that the cunning and the bully gained at the expense of the law-abiding and the conscientious.

Even so, the attractions of rationing were superficial. It seemed to work fairly well for the few years of war or siege in standardised commodities like tea, margarine and bacon (even then 'need' was measured by crude criteria of age, etc.). But it was ludicrously unsuitable for unstandardisable commodities where tastes vary, like shirts or shoes. And money had to be partially restored by allotting 'points' (a form of cash) and 'point' values (a form of prices), otherwise everyone would have had to have basically the same (as Russian women's coats are now). That is the socialism for which Mr Foot hoped for votes in 1983. He had lost touch with the people. His successors talk about listening to the people, but that would paralyse socialism, which must work (allocate resources) from the top.

A second feature of siege-time socialism was that in centralised decisions on large-scale essential investment, 'the emergency' rode roughshod over minorities, who were simply ignored and coerced into accepting what the decisions, supposedly based on majority interests, laid down. The more decisions are centralised, made by political bodies, the more socialism ignores individuals, small groups, local interests, who have little or no democratic voice in the vast machinery of 'planning'. Socialists say that in war, centralised decisions make for efficiency. They also make for more coercion, in which more and more people count for nothing. That is socialism; it runs more and more human life by politics: party politics. Did Mr Foot think he would win votes from individuals flattened by socialism? He discovered they want to own their homes. They will want much more influence over their private lives—all incompatible with socialism.

War required all necessary resources—manpower, womanpower, equipment, buildings, land, savings—to be mobilised for defence and attack and therefore removed from all other purposes, which had to come second.

All this could, technically, have been done by taking purchasing power away from people by taxation and spending it on the armed forces, war factories, food-growing and so on. Any shortfall would have been made good by borrowing from the people or abroad. The supply of 'peace'-goods left for non-war consumption would fall, their prices would rise, and the demand for them would fall away. The demand for war-goods would grow and their production would expand. That is how the minor wars of the nineteenth century were financed and equipped: without much economic disturbance, loss of political or other liberties, or financial inflation.

No country in modern times has mobilised resources for major wars by this method because it is too leisurely, and in wartime they suddenly become scarce, valuable and vital enough to be bought at all costs because the consequence—defeat—is worth all possible sacrifices. So the transition from peace to war economy is organised by authority armed with emergency powers to save time above all. As in all crises, time is vital and to hell with the cost.

But the cost is borne, and the sacrifices are made. Preferences for peace-time pursuits are willingly sacrificed precisely because there is a crisis that demands fast-acting emergency measures. But the willingness to accept them is created by our instinctive understanding that, since emergencies are by definition not permanent, the measures they require are correspondingly *temporary*. The willingness to abandon rights and accept sacrifices might be very different if they were likely to be lost for ever. But that is what socialism means—in war or peace.

Taxation itself would take time to raise and be diverted to pay for war production. Saving could be encouraged by patriotic appeals—as they were during the Second World War—but even they would not suffice fast enough. So the required shortfall in purchasing power to pay for armaments would have to be printed. That would—and did—create inflation (though not so virulent as in the last ten years since the Heath-led inflationary printing of money in 1972–3). And inflation would have been arbitrary in its results on incomes, it would have put some everyday commodities beyond the reach of people not caught up in the war economy, and it would therefore require controls.

Then again, offering higher pay in the armed services would have been too slow—and arbitrary—as the means of building up the army, navy and air forces. So voluntary recruitment was soon replaced by conscription, which the distinguished liberal (in the classical sense) Professor Lord Robbins once argued would be justified on the ground that 'when the safety of the state is seriously threatened', that is, in the emergency of war, taxes to facilitate defence could be paid in kind (personal services) as well as in money.

Labour to make armaments, as well as soldiers to fire them in battle, could have been mobilised by offering higher pay than in non-war production. And to a large degree it was. But again freedom of choice in the labour market would have worked too slowly, and it was reinforced by direction of labour—of young men down the mines ('Bevin-boys'), women to munitions factories and so on.

Raw materials, plant, vehicles, land and other material resources could have been attracted by monetary inducements, but the mass of equipment that had to be transferred was too large for the relaxed but more leisurely 'method of freedom', as Walter Lippmann, the American writer, called it in a famous book. So it had to be commandeered and directed to war use and sometimes prohibited to peace purposes. Again, more choice, freedoms and liberties were suspended to avoid defeat and risk the more permanent loss of liberties if Hitler had invaded and subjugated Britain.

Then, to induce firms to increase production of war materials quickly, it is simplest to pay them a price that covers their costs plus a profit margin to cover risks. This 'cost-plus' is not the best method, since it accepts 'costs' as unalterable, leaves room for inflation of costs and is probably wasteful of industrial capacity and tax ('public') expenditure. But it is the *quickest* method. And in war *time* counts above all else. Prices are therefore fixed as 'cost plus'.

The prices of necessary consumer goods are also fixed because the alternative is to let demand raise them beyond the income of some people. Profits would also rise conspicuously; they could be taxed, but probably with adverse effects on incentives. So prices are fixed and distribution is based on rationing—replacing real but unequal money with artificial but equal money.

Once the 'method of freedom' is suspended in the war sectors of the economy, controls and rationing have to be applied in other sectors because controlling supplies and prices in some sectors affects supplies and prices in the other sectors from which supplies are obtained. The ultimate reason is that total war requires increasingly total control to lose no *time* in ensuring the flow of resources to the war industries and the flow of output from them.

But if controls to remove freedom were essential in war, why did they succeed? To be effective they would have to be obeyed faithfully even where they conflicted with immediate individual interest, as they often did. Were the required products and services produced in the right quantities, in the right qualities, sizes, shapes, at the right times, in the right places? The answer is not easy. War production was not simply a question of producing 'shells', 'tanks', 'aeroplanes', 'uniforms'. *Quantity* was only one requirement. The others were *quality*, *place*, *time*. That is the trouble with measurements of the efficiency or output of socialist economies: they can produce figures of quantities—so many pairs of shoes—but they are not very good at producing figures of *effectiveness*, or *satisfactions*, or *utilities*, which means quality, place, time, and so on because they do not produce to consumer requirements but to central planners' orders. In peacetime consumers may have to wear ill-fitting shoes of designs they don't like and lump it, as often in Russia. In wartime, delivery of the wrong shells to the wrong place at the wrong time can mean annihilation of an army and defeat, as sometimes happened in the highly centralised German army.

The argument that has raged between economists on whether it is possible to calculate and 'plan' desired required production in socialist economies without prices—whether in Russia in peace or Britain at war—applied to the 1939–45 siege economy. Although the British war economy seemed to work—the arms were produced, battles were won, the enemy was finally defeated—it was fearfully inefficient and wasteful, because it was based largely on *guesses* at the centre about *which* shells, guns, tanks, aeroplanes, were required *where* and *when*. The grim reality is that the war was won because the allied war economies were slightly less *inefficient* than the top-heavy, over-centralised, inflexible, brittle German war machine. The war was won not *because* of temporary emergency socialism, but *in spite* of it.

The real reason for victory was the sense of common danger which induced individuals to forego their private anxieties, sink their differences, and sacrifice their comfort, their homes, and ultimately their lives. Yet some people, even in war, 'worked' the system to their personal advantage by under-the-counter deals, black market activities, and corruption. But in general the common danger induced the British to observe rules and regulations against their immediate private interests. Again, it was not the socialised economy run from the centre but the sense of shared danger and resistance to evil, nothing to do with Foot's socialism, that produced the resources for victory.

This sense of solidarity also restrained the 'fiddling' (extra butter, rashers, nylons) that disfigured the British war effort on the home front (and even in the armed services, where 'scrounging' was endemic). In a *peacetime* regulated socialist Britain it would spread like wildfire throughout the whole economic system, as it has in all socialist countries from Russia to India.

The structure of controls was in place to direct supplies of services where they were required, but they had to be accepted as necessary in emergency, that is, for a limited period, to enable them to work. If there were not this voluntary acceptance, the system may have had to be as repressive and brutal as it was in wartime German national socialism and is now in peacetime Russian communism. Few British people were free of mobilisation, conscription, direction of labour, rationing, licensing or other wartime regulations.

This is the socialism that Mr Foot says approaches nearest to the ideal he has in mind for the British now. If it was acceptable in war, and seemed to work, more or less, with everyone in a job, everyone with his/her ration of meat, butter, orange-juice, shoes, stockings, why not in peace?

This is characteristic socialist thinking. People are units to be supplied with the 'essentials' of life, not individuals with minds of their own, with hopes, dislikes, preferences, feelings, sensitivities, tolerances, even hates. The simplified standardised food and clothing of war were accepted because they were secondary to resisting defeat and because they were temporary. The alternatives were: sacrifice or die. The British accepted the barest minimum to keep everyday life going only because of the overriding danger.

It is crass naivety to suppose this is what the British would accept in peacetime today. But it is splendid that Mr Foot's successors, even if unintentionally, should say clearly what 'socialism' in peacetime would mean for everyday living. At last the people have real 'socialism' to judge. The socialism of Kinnock, Heffer, Hattersley or Shore is the socialism of Foot dressed up in fine language to disguise its coercive weaponry.

Their socialism would reproduce in the 1980s the austerities, sacrifices, rules, regulations, orders, prohibitions, rationing, licensing, directions, mobilisations, conscriptions of 1939–45. It would make life comfortable, easy and simple for the politicians, planners, bureaucrats, officials, but a straitjacket for the people. The planners in peacetime would, without guides to individual consumers' wishes, have to guess; and they would make a hash of it. The task of scientific socialism, carefully discovering people's 'needs', would dissolve into quarrels for the spoils between organised interests. But no-one would know because they could, and would, hide their hash. That would make Britain Two Nations with a vengeance: the practitioners and the victims of socialism.

Worst of all, once this system were foisted on Britain it would take an earthquake to dislodge. Even now, if you go into any public or private place, the chances are that two out of seven are in the planning—the socialist—machinery. Think of the people with 'public' jobs—from administrators to cooks and porters—who would resist any effort to make them really accountable in *everyday practice* to the wishes of the public, as distinct from the phoney accountability of Westminster or Town Hall.

That is Michael Foot's socialism in practice—official.

Whatever his understanding of liberty, Michael Foot was held, even by some Conservative opponents, like Enoch Powell, to be a great House of Commons man, sensitive to its importance in preserving liberty. He could take a lesson from one of the greatest Commons men,

William Pitt, who two hundred years ago in 1783 said in the House of Commons:

> Necessity is the plea for every infringement of human freedom. It is the argument of tyrants; it is the creed of slaves.

Why should the socialism of Kinnock work differently?

3

The Socialist Guilty Secret

The strongest case made by some socialists is that people are not merely individuals who live for themselves but members of a community who affect one another for good or ill—as residents in a street or village, as pupils in a school, doctors and staff in a hospital, employees at a workbench or factory and so on. In everyday economic life these effects of social or legal contracts between two parties on other people—'third parties'—are known as social costs or benefits, or external effects, or in economic language, 'externalities',

The socialist argument is that people cannot be allowed to make arrangements with each other without taking into account the third-party effects—either compensating people they harm (for example, by smoke or noise) or claiming compensation from those they benefit (by providing amenities such as coach stations near their homes). In principle, there is a good argument for both. It has been countered that the theory is questionable or fallacious.* And it has also been maintained that subsidies or taxes are not the best way to compensate or charge third parties. † But let us suppose these objections can be repulsed. We are then left with the socialist argument that if economic life is conceived or planned or run by the state, it can more easily take externalities into account.

The obvious weakness of this argument is that the very action taken by the state to remove external or social costs itself creates indirect external or other harmful effects that are part and parcel of the socialist system. Yet even the most sophisticated and scholarly socialists rarely, if ever, analyse them. Indeed they hardly ever refer to them at all. Why? Is there a subconscious anxiety to conceal that state action has all-too-obvious

*Professor S. N. Cheung, *The Myth of Social Cost*, IEA, 1978.
† Professor S. C. Littlechild, *The Fallacy of the Mixed Economy*, IEA, 1980.

costs as well as loudly-trumpeted benefits—or at least *promises* of benefits?

What are the costs of socialism—or at least the main ones? For, however impressive the case for socialism, socialists should at least tell us *all* its effects—adverse as well as favourable—if people urged to accept or demand socialism are to take a fully-informed decision to support or oppose it. In other words, what *price* are we being asked to pay for the benefits, small or large, real or supposed, of socialism?

I suggest, very briefly, with only a few lines on each rather than a full discussion, that the main 'externalities' and other necessary consequences or disadvantages of socialism are at least twenty in number. Readers will no doubt add others from their personal experience in various walks of life.

(1) Socialism requires much higher taxation than liberal market economies, not only to finance the much wider range of services— national, regional or local—but also for their administration. In the UK, taxation (including all levies of varying kinds) takes not far from half of earnings. Some calculations go down to 45 per cent, others up to 60 per cent. The costs of administering the assessment, collection and spending of all this money is enormous in total. But it is usually very much understated in the official statistics, even in the UK, where official accuracy and honesty is higher than in some other Western capitalist, and certainly than in all socialist, countries. The official statistic for the administrative cost of the National Health Service, for example, is published as around 6 per cent. But it excludes the 'bucks' it passes to industry, doctors and others to do much of its clerical and accounting records, the losses of time (which means money) it imposes on patients who have to wait for hours in surgeries, hospitals, etc., the inconvenience, if not disruption, it imposes on industry by calling on a key man for cold (non-urgent) surgery who may dislocate a working group and endanger a contract, the time lost by families in travelling miles to see in-patients in distant hospitals built large because they were thought more economic but with no regard for the 'external' effects on third parties. (One NHS technocrat, a Vice-Chancellor of a University, proposed that NHS hospitals have 2000 beds, or even up to 5000. The NHS has discovered— by observing private hospitals—that the best size is around 250–350 beds.)

(2) Because of its unnecessarily high taxation, socialism imposes stronger disincentives to earn, save, invest, take risks, start up new firms,

export to unfamiliar markets. Whether the taxation is for necessary 'public goods' (see (12) below) or for unnecessary use of manpower in overstaffed schools, overmanned uneconomic steel mills, trains or coal pits, etc., it has exactly the same damaging effects on individuals and on the economy as a whole in loss of output of goods and services that could raise living standards, especially for the poorer.

(3) Socialism requires larger bureaucracies than other systems. The insensitivity, arrogance, and other faults of bureaucrats—from the Whitehall Sir Humphreys of *Yes, Minister* to the young clerk at the local Job Centre—are common experience. But their sins are worse than that. Many tax-paid employees perform direct personal services for the citizen—from nurses in geriatric wards to home helps. It cannot be said of all of them that they are concerned more for the feelings of their charges than about fulfilling their duties according to the rules in the book so that they can accept their pay with good conscience. We have tolerated cant about the 'public service' of 'public servants' for too long.

(4) Socialism is indeed most at fault in personal services where it should be most sensitive—'caring' or 'compassionate' in the well-worn language of the social worker or sociologist. For since a socialist system can try to demonstrate its efficiency, or at least, performance only by *quantitative* 'indicators'—so many patients treated per week, etc.—it can say nothing about the *quality* of its services: there is no way of measuring its clients' satisfaction or dissatisfaction, because many clients would fear giving their opinion if they were dissatisfied. In any event, the system is not primarily interested in quality, since it does not risk losing its customers if they are dissatisfied. Little wonder the system is not interested in their opinions, and instinctively resists reforms that would transfer the balance of decision-making in personal services from the suppliers to the consumers. The poorest teachers especially fear the school voucher, which would make schools more responsive to parents' opinions, wishes and judgments about their own children; the better teachers, like the best providers of services, prefer customers who choose them in preference to others.

(5) Socialism gives power to officials to usurp the influence and authorities of parents in families. Parents have limited power to help their children in education, medical care, even housing (where one in three families live in a home they cannot shape to their requirements or preferences). And children sense that their parents have diminished influence on their lives; juvenile delinquency is one result.

(6) Socialism is the biggest thief of time the world has known. Its faults of inefficiency—goods of the wrong sort in the wrong place—are hidden by making people wait. Socialism claims to make no mistakes; they can all be concealed in time. This may be the most damaging 'externality' of socialism, and would require a book to explain in detail.

(7) Socialism denies a choice even where technical conditions make a choice practicable. I have discussed this failing in other chapters.

(8) Socialism provides 'public' services that are almost always wholly or largely monopolies. It is the unanswerable objection to monopoly in all forms, 'public' or private, that it opposes or slows down innovation. But the danger is worse with socialised than with private monopolies, because the state can more easily obstruct new enterprises to save its 'public' undertakings, its powers, or at least its face from the demonstration that state activity is not necessarily the most efficient. Conservative councillors are as obstructive as Labour (or Liberal) councillors in persisting with long-standing local services such as abattoirs, car-parking, libraries, etc. that could be performed more efficiently by competing suppliers. But they do not know, because they shirk comparison by competition.

(9) Socialised services are supplied in response to the strength of the 'cultural' power used to gain access to them—from accent and family background to occupational links and political patronage. These cultural powers are 'regressive' in effect; they tend to redistribute services away from the poorer and weaker to the richer and stronger. This defect of socialism would fill another book.

(10) Socialism has intensified the potential damage to the public from the power of the strike threat from 'public' sector trade unions. British readers hardly require examples from recent and current events in schools, hospitals, water, refuse-collection, social work, railways, social insurance payments, etc.

(11) Socialism, as in Yugoslavia but also in the UK, replaces consumer sovereignty by syndicalism in worker self-management which, naturally and inevitably, takes a short-term view and underinvests for a future in which they may have no stake by overpaying themselves in current wages. (The best work on this subject is by Dr Ljubo Sirc, of the University of Glasgow.)

(12) Socialism stimulates social conflict, religious sectarianism and regional separatism by empowering political majorities to subjugate minorities, groups or individuals in services that are *not* public goods.

The *diktat* of majority decisions is unavoidable only for public goods—defence, law, order, public health, local roads, etc. The Catholics of Northern Ireland cannot outvote the Protestants, the Welsh or Scotsmen cannot outvote the Englishmen, the Sikhs or Pakistanis (who want their daughters in single-sex schools) cannot outvote the local 'WASPS' in services that government does *not* have to supply. Socialism is a device for creating melting-pots *by force* that in time become seething cauldrons of racial disharmony and antipathy. Forced mixing—as Aneurin Bevan tried in council housing estates, or as was tried by bussing schoolchildren in the USA—is as obnoxious and doomed to fail as forced feeding.

(13) Socialism intervenes more in private, social and economic life than any other system. Its ability to influence groups of citizens as voters, taxpayers, workers, and in virtually all capacities gives it the power to benefit or damage them. Groups therefore organise themselves to press their case or claims by deputations, demonstrations, marches, sit-ins, strikes, boycotts, refusal to pay taxes. To minimise the dislocation to the economy, government then tends to yield to the best-organised groups that can cause most disruption if their case is ignored or their claim rejected. That is, it responds to the amount of 'noise' made by disgruntled or disaffected groups and not to what are often the larger *numbers* of citizens who initially do not, or cannot, use these forms of public pressure. After a time they can see that if government yields only to 'noise', the 'quiet' people must take to the streets if their case is to be heard. Society becomes an arena for warring factions in which the noise of protest prevails over the merits of the argument. The interventionist state transforms society into a bear-garden. And socialism can suppress the frictions it foments only by successive enlargement of repression, censorship, imprisonment and (in its communist forms), if judicial murder would outrage the outside world, incarceration as 'hospital' inmates.

(14) Socialism tends to breed corruption—not least in local government, where staff with middling salaries have the power to grant or deny permits, licences, and other permissions that may mean prosperity or bankruptcy to local firms and life or death to the men who run them. (The capitalist solution uses the market in forms such as auctioning licences, etc.—as the Hungarian economist, Tibor Liska, proposed before he was silenced.)

(15) Socialism creates vested interests that resist change. In the short run it becomes technically backward. In the medium run it tries to replace innovation by industrial espionage in capitalist countries. In the

long run, when the arrears behind capitalist technology becomes widely known, socialism provokes revolution.

(16) Socialism has prevented the development of earlier forms and the emergence of new forms of voluntary, mutual, co-operative enterprise in production, marketing, financing (health insurance) and saving. This is a subject for yet a third book—or two or three more.

(17) Socialism in one country, or a group of countries, in an expanding world economy where men, money and ideas can move freely, can be sustained in the last resort (as the Communist forms of socialism suggest) only by coercion, force, tyranny, incarceration or legalised murder.

(18) Socialism in one country—Britain—is *national* socialism, which is impracticable in an open European or world economy. *That* is essentially why British socialists want to leave Europe, not the hocus-pocus reasons of intolerable restrictions on British standards. Socialism in Britain would isolate it from the rest of the Western world.

(19) Socialism rations by official decree, which, as India and other countries show, proliferates corruption.

(20) Socialism and its taxation incites high borrowing, high deficits, high interest rates and the temptation to print money, which provokes inflation, which socialism pretends to prevent by *suppression*.

I have little doubt that this list would be extended without difficulty to fifty or a hundred.

Whether it is a good product or poor, socialism has a high price that the British would not pay. But no-one can tell. For its worst fault—number 101?—is that *socialism conceals its worst consequences by burning the books or liquidating its book-keepers*.

4

The Sad Saga of Incorrigible Socialism

It is time to sum up the sad saga of socialism. Brave, able, wise, saintly men (who trace socialism back to early Christianity) have held out the vision of universal brotherhood, of selfless sharing, with injustice abandoned, poverty abolished. For decades going back to almost a century, the poor and the lowly have been raised up by *hopes* of amelioration and plenty.

But young people and students have had their idealism harnessed to a mirage. Men and women who would wish to live a life of selflessness have been led to advocate a system in which the quest for power is easiest for the selfish, the power-hungry, the autocrat and the tyrant. Men who have had little more than the gift of the gab to promise largesse at the expense of the unsuspecting citizen—not least in local government, who would not be entrusted with the small savings of pensioners—have acquired the power to distribute millions and billions of money with no definable responsibility or accountability to anyone—the electorate at large, Parliament or the local citizen.

To varying degrees the deficiencies and evils of socialism *in practice*, in contrast to its hopes and promises in speeches and manifestos, party political broadcasts or Parliament, are common to every form in which we have seen it round the world so far—from the mild forms in Sweden and Austria to the venal forms in the USSR, East Germany and Bulgaria. The case against socialism is not that it has faults from which other systems are free. Capitalism in its varying forms—from the mixed economy of Britain to the purest form in Switzerland—has faults that are, or were once, sometimes special to itself and others that are common with those of socialism. The difference is that they are not inherent where found in capitalism and so can be removed more easily than from socialism. In a word, capitalism is corrigible, socialism is incorrigible.

It is not difficult to identify the faults of capitalism that are peculiar to it.

It was strongly maintained by socialists in the nineteenth and early twentieth centuries that they would not recur in socialism. Yet in almost every form of socialism we have observed in every continent they have reappeared in one form or another and, even worse, in a form that is far more difficult to dislodge.

Let the main defects or results of economic failure be listed—in a broadly descending order according to the emphasis they are given in socialist propaganda.

(1) Poverty/living standards/security.
(2) Inequality/social cohesion/community spirit/third-party social costs, quality of life.
(3) Accountability/involvement/participation.
(4) Inequity/injustice/privilege.
(5) Unemployment/inflation.
(6) Stability/fluctuations.
(7) Individual freedom/liberty/coercion.
(8) Efficiency/inefficiency.
(9) Monopoly.
(10) Corruption/secrecy.

I shall argue that elements of all these abuses are found in both socialism and capitalism but they are more difficult to remove under socialism. And in all this discussion I shall be concerned not with what experts, or elitists—whether socialists, social democrats, liberals, or conservatives—think is best for the people, but with judging systems that best enable the *people*, with the advantage of experience and guidance, to decide the lives *they* want to live.

(1) Poverty, living standards, security

From all the attention focused by the professional propagandists of poverty, you might suppose that poverty was the product of capitalism and easily solved under socialism. At an encounter in 1981 in the Chapel at Windsor Castle under the auspices of the St George's Trust, I told Professor Peter Townsend (the Essex sociologist) that he had confused the whole question and made its solutions more difficult by distorting the word 'poverty' into meaning any condition in which some people had lower income than the average. If this was poverty, half (or even more than half) of the British people would be described as 'poor' even though they were richer than the masses in Africa, Asia and South America. And his solution—transferring income from the 'rich' to the 'poor'—would go no part of the way to abolishing poverty.

People are 'poor' if they lack the essentials of civilised living. The only solutions are then immediate 'first-aid' to provide the essentials by other people, and in the long run advice, teaching and example on how to equip the 'poor' with skills that would enable them to produce for themselves at least the civilised essentials.

This is the only long-run solution under any system in the world. I maintain that the poor have a better chance of being raised out of poverty in capitalism than they have under socialism. Basically the reason is not that people in capitalism are more compassionate in the stage of 'first-aid'—although I see no signs of more compassion in socialist countries round the world—but that capitalism is *more productive* and can produce the funds both for 'first-aid' and for long-run re-training and re-equipment.

(2) Inequality, social cohesion, community spirit, third-party social costs, quality of life

Inequality may be wider in some forms of capitalism in some periods than in socialist countries, but capitalism contains a mechanism making for equality that socialism lacks. There are two aspects of inequality; in earning and in spending. Equality in earning spreads upward spontaneously from the bottom in capitalism as people *move* as they themselves wish from jobs, occupations, homes, towns and areas where incomes are lower to where they are higher. And the freer markets can be made, the more easily people can move. Equality in socialism can be created by the state but only by the opposite methods of coercion—*prevention* of movement between the layers of a rigid hierarchial structure in industry and politics, limitation of numbers in higher-paid occupations (which destroys the price signals of higher earnings that indicate job vacancies to remove scarcity of supply of labour), vindictive taxation of relatively high earners.

Inequality is more deeply ingrained in socialism and more difficult to moderate than in capitalism. In socialism access to services is largely determined by influence—based on family origins, language, accent, temperament, character, social connections, occupational links. Even if prices are fixed by government with the intention of making goods and services available to people with the lowest incomes, they are ignored or evaded if they do not, by chance, equate supply and demand. If, as is most common, they are fixed too low, demand outruns supply, with the results of queuing, favouritism, secret deals, grey markets, black markets, corruption and worse. In this contest, the strong in influence outbid the weak.

In capitalism there are also inequalities of access—based on differences in income or wealth. But it is easier to even up differences in financial power—by redistributive taxation, cash grants, a reverse income tax, earmarked purchasing power (vouchers) and other devices.

Evidence round the world clearly indicates that the natural urge to self-improvement produces more *spontaneous* equality in the USA, Canada, the Netherlands, Scandinavia, Australasia and elsewhere than the *enforced* equality in the socialist countries (where shops and housing and colleges are reserved for the upper political or official strata of the state machinery, the favoured intellectuals or writers, the party loyalists, the secret police, not for the proletariat, for whom the socialist revolution, we should recall, was engineered).

Difference of any kind can provoke social dissension. But there is a world of difference between the inequalities in societies where men and women feel that they can improve themselves by learning skills, hard work, attending to the wants of consumers (in markets) and the jealousy, or resignation, in hierarchical societies where the lower orders know they will never be able to improve themselves by such efforts. The difference is between the hope based on emulation in capitalism—well attested by evidence around the world—and the destruction of hope based on envy—and again amply attested by the evidence from the third of the world run as 'socialism'.

(3) Accountability, involvement, participation

One of the saddest illusions fostered by socialists is that representative institutions in socialism will ensure that elected bodies—committees, boards, commissions—are truly responsive and accountable to the people who elected them. Hence the continuing call by even moderate Labour politicians like Eric Varley for the 'public' control of the important, basic community services. The truth is sad, because it has induced the peoples of all democracies to abandon their powers of decision over their lives to handfuls of men (and women)—half a dozen, a score, even a few hundred as in the British Parliament—who are given massive power over them and massive amounts of money—millions and billions—to provide them with services in which they have no say, do not want, and also, into the bargain, deprive them of the services they do want.

Think of these examples:

How many British people would willingly have wanted their children to go to 2000-pupil schools?

How many sick people would willingly have gone into 2000-bed hospitals?

How many people would willingly have wanted to live in 2000-tenant tower blocks?

Yet these are the latest specimens of the work (sometimes called 'social engineering') of democratic bodies elected by the sovereign people. And what did the faithful representatives do? Did they consult their true masters, the people? They proceeded to appoint opiniated educational sociologists, hospital planners or architects, and town planners and let them run amok, spending billions of the peoples' money on vast buildings to house large numbers of schoolchildren, patients and tenants that the people would have not chosen themselves. But once the buildings were erected, the children, patients and tenants were drafted with little chance of escape. That is 'public' control of services for the masses—democratic, accountable, participatory public services that 'involved' the people: the object, end-product and 'glory' of socialism in real, everyday, life. The socialist textbooks, pamphlets, poems, weeklies, monthlies, broadcasts, manifestoes say nothing about real-life socialism.

These three examples are characteristic of the way in which post-war democracy has *mis*interpreted the peoples' wants, worries and wishes. That is how the mass of the welfare state, nationalised industries, public corporations and local authorities have worked, with the added gloss of a Parent–Teacher Association here, a 'Consumer Council' there. Whatever the theory or intention of parliamentary democracy, representative government, it has failed to represent—reflect—the wishes of the people. Poor old honest Abe Lincoln would denounce this prostitution of his principle that democracy meant government *of* the people, *by* the people, *for* the people. In the real world socialism, even if called democratic socialism or social democracy, has twisted it into government of the glib, by the officious, for the adroit: of the busy, by the bossy, for the bully.

I draw a conclusion that will shock many who hopefully accepted the post-war consensus that government would know what to do, and would by and large do the right thing. My conclusion is that, however suitable it may have been until the inter-war years, representative democracy is now no longer equipped to interpret, represent and respond to public wishes, public opinion or public preferences. We shall in Britain—social democrats, liberal democrats or Christian democrats—have to accept that the Age of Representative Democracy is over. It has been outdated by technical progress and social advance.

Let me explain. Representative democracy in parliamentary government is still required to provide services we all want but cannot organise in any other way—defence against external danger, security against internal danger to life or belongings, law courts to uphold the law on these matters and police to prevent it being broken. There are also secondary services that government has to supply—local (but not national) roads, environmental health protection, possibly research from which all may gain but which few individuals could finance. And that is about all. For the rest, government is simply incompetent—not equipped to discover the peoples' wants, inefficient in supplying them and, worst of all, has no incentive to provide them faithfully. But at least in public goods it is a necessary evil.

For all the other services that government now supplies, 'representative' government—which is socialism in practice if not in name—is a fraud. Most of all other services—fuel and transport, education and health, housing and culture, refuse-collection and firefighting—we could supply far better and far cheaper by discovering among ourselves what we want and letting the most suitable people supply it. We could do this in all sorts of ways that government in Britain has stopped or suppressed or frowned on—by ordinary commercial buying and selling, by starting voluntary enterprises of co-operatives of teachers or doctors, by mutual exchange of services with no passage of money at all. There should be no favours for each method—and more yet unknown and untried—but also no restrictions. Let them all go ahead and see which performs best. You may think that means a drastic slash at the volume of government. You would be right. Three economists of repute* recently judged that 90 per

* Professor C. D. Foster, Richard Jackman and Morris Perlman of the London School of Economics, in *Local Government Financing in a Unitary State*, Allen and Unwin, 1980.

cent of local government expenditure was on services it did not have to supply! For the country as a whole I put the proportion at 70 per cent.

And that is the only system of co-operation, commercial or non-commercial, inside or outside the market of buying and selling, that can, and should be supported by democrats of all kinds, social, liberal, or conservative.

Provided they all produce goods and services according to the wishes or preferences of their consumers—which includes themselves—let productive enterprises be owned, run and controlled by any one man or woman, or two or more partners, or groups, small, large or medium, buying and selling, exchanging, borrowing and lending, swapping, giving and taking. Let people work—produce—for as much as they can get or as little as satisfies them. But they must make things wanted by other people—and wanted enough to pay for them.

Who knows how the system would look after it had settled down? I should expect a smallish 'mutual' section of exchange by barter, a larger co-operative section of voluntary groups for production for their own use (as in housing and farming, but little else), and probably the largest sector of vigorous market buying and selling of goods and services, with new suppliers starting up or dropping out according to changing techniques, social habits and personal preferences.

I call this system a free economy. You could call it a voluntary society. Others might call it a 'free-for-all'. What's in a name? But it would be of the *people*, by the *people*, for the *people*. And one name it could *not* have is socialism.

(4) Inequity, injustice, privilege

These are three terms generally used to express the sense of outrage created by the advantages enjoyed by some that seem to have no connection with their contribution to society, mankind, their neighbours. They are among the supposed arguments for socialism on the ground that they are common in capitalism.

As with inequality and poverty, my reply is not only that they are more common in socialism than in capitalism, but that they are even more difficult to eradicate. And for much the same reasons.

A central distinction is that capitalism is relatively open or mobile and socialism relatively hierarchical. Socialism must be more hierarchical because it cannot be planned from the centre (even when administered in the regions) if people are able to move about unpredictably and, so it will seem to the planners, arbitrarily, to suit passing moods or illogical fancies. As teachers, faced with the revolutionary idea that they should be answerable to parents (rather than to local authority officials), are apt to respond: 'How could we then plan ahead?' (2500 private schools in Britain have learned how to do precisely that).

In contrast, capitalism is not planned from the centre but (except for public goods) at the periphery through innumerable arrangements, exchanges, understandings, undertakings or formal contracts between buyers and sellers of products, labour, advice, or, as emphasised above, formal co-operative ventures or informal exchanges, or barter.

Inequity, injustice, privilege is more common in socialism because position, function, power are assigned or legitimised by superior authority. They are therefore more difficult to eat into by movement of people from positions with less privilege to those with more privilege. That is the essence of the reason for the deeper, long-lasting and more resented inequalities of socialism.

In Part 2, Brian Crozier traces the development of socialism in the USSR but the Soviet experiment is so central to my argument that I cannot ignore it.

The pages of *The Russians*,* the three-year study of the everyday lives of the individual inhabitants of the USSR by a sympathetic rather than hostile writer, are chock-a-block with examples of people with power, national, regional or local, who use it to obtain favours, goods, services, access to the better shops, restaurants, forms of travel, even education and medicine for themselves, their spouses, their children, their parents, their friends, to buy off people they fear, or simply to barter with others with influence to exchange. Much of the same is true of all countries where buying and selling in markets (official or driven underground) is replaced by power to allocate and ration materials, or to deny or demand favours in return. None of this is new to observers of socialism in day-to-day real life, but professional socialists are strangely silent.

Socialism does not replace the formal buying and selling of capitalism, or the informal exchange or swapping. It replaces the voluntary exchanges of capitalism, from which both parties gain because the

---

* Hedrick Smith, *The Russians*, Ballantine Books, New York, 1976; Eleventh printing 1981.

bargains they arrive at are voluntary, by the arbitrary deals in socialism between people with widely varying power based on political influence, connections and bargaining leverage. Again socialists who want to know how socialism works in practice can read the torrent of cases in the testimony of Konstantin Simis, a Russian defence lawyer*.

(5) **Unemployment, inflation**

Especially in recent years, the advocates of socialism have claimed that at least it avoids the hardship of unemployment and inflation. This is yet another figment of the socialist imagination, or another symptom of socialists' failure to understand how socialist countries work, or another revelation of the ignorance of how socialist statistics are compiled, and for what purpose.

First, 'unemployment' and 'inflation' are impossible to interpret, still less measure, except in an open capitalist society. In socialism the full-time activity of every man (and woman) of working age does not mean there is no unemployment in any significant sense of this term, only that everyone is engaged in doing something. But *activity* is not *performance*. The inmates of capitalist prisons sewing mailbags may be better employed than the builders of socialist houses that no-one wants to live in or that collapse after a few years. (There are plenty more examples in *The Russians*.) 'Employment' must mean producing something that someone else wants and will pay for. In capitalism there is at least a mechanism, the market, for attaching a value to such products. It is very imperfect (as discussed in Chapter 3), but at least it is a more or less certain if only approximate guide. But in socialism (unless it makes use of markets, which only some socialists understand it must, and many socialists in Britain do not even realise that it must have a value-assessing mechanism of some sort, much as they may dislike it), the measure of 'useful' employment is decided by the planners who, by chance, may guess right but who mostly bungle their job, so that the wrong goods are delivered in the wrong places, in the wrong sizes, shapes and qualities.

Socialist statistics on inflation no more indicate the movement in prices reflecting the real underlying conditions of supply and demand than socialist statistics of employment are indicators of wasted labour.

* *USSR: Secrets of a Corrupt Society,* J. M. Dent, 1982.

The difference is not that capitalist countries have suffered from inflation and socialist countries have not, but that capitalist countries have *published* their statistics of inflation and socialist countries have not.

Socialist countries can, moreover, suppress the extent of inflation by price controls, lowering quality, and other devices. Yet to some extent even the socialist countries cannot entirely conceal their failings. One piece of evidence that inflation is suppressed in the USSR, for example, is that the official rate of exchange between the rouble and sterling (and the dollar, the deutschmark, the Swiss franc, the French franc) is much lower than the free market value. No wonder that Russians in the USSR offer the visitor many more roubles for overseas currencies than the 'official' (or rather artificial, meaningless), rates of exchange.

And the probable unemployment statistic in socialist countries? I would say that if unemployment is officially 12 per cent in the UK (3 million out of a workforce of 25 million), it is probably nearer 8 per cent, since perhaps a million or more of the officially 'unemployed' are hard at work, by day or night, in the ironically named 'underground' to which the British contorted system of high taxation on earnings has driven the normally law-abiding British. As a corresponding measure of the Soviet labour force directed to production of goods and services desired by the population rather than in relatively useless bureaucratic activity I would put the rate of unemployment at 50 per cent. (Average earnings in the USSR are less than a half of incomes in the UK.)

(6) Fluctuations and stability

Again much the same observations apply. Fluctuation and instability in capitalism are an open book—published currently by the main countries, the OECD, other organisations, and much analysed, dissected and savoured by the socialist critics of capitalism in the British and overseas press, television, the Church and opinionated non-economists among academics, especially sociologists.

These critics usually say little (or nothing) of fluctuations and instability in the socialist countries. Are we to suppose there is none because the socialist countries say so? Are we asked to believe that their statistics are faithful records of events, not intellectual and political propaganda? Are there no economic fluctuations because Comecon publishes no verifiable statistics?

It is no use looking for the evidence of socialist instability and fluctuations among the statistics. The truth is blurted out, or ferreted out by chance observers. Here is one morsel that combines all or many of the concealed components of failure: the writer is Hedrick Smith in *The Russians*:

> ... jimmying ['exploiting', 'working', 'prostituting'] the Plan went on everywhere ... one dissident economist, writing under a pseudonym [so much for the free speech in socialism loudly claimed by British socialists] and buried somewhere in the state administration, circulated an underground document showing how in category after category the economy had fallen short of the 1966–1970 Five-Year-Plan targets even though overall growth of national income had met planned objectives. *Hidden inflation covered up most of the shortfall. (My italics and insertions in square brackets.)*

Official lies designed to conceal failure can be traced again by chance knowledge. A pamphlet near the end of 1971 called *Free Thought* compared published Soviet statistics, showing that from 1966 to 1970 only 25 per cent of the 'planned' number of cars, 40 per cent of tractors, 50 per cent of paper and cheese, 70 per cent of electric power, 71 per cent of steel, etc. had been produced, despite claims in 1971 that all major targets of the Plan had been fulfilled.

Even these shortfall figures may be suspect. They may be too high or too low, because the Plan targets are not, of course, based on scientific estimates of the optimum production from the available resources. They may be put too high to goad the workers into harder work, in which case the shortfall is overstated. Or they may be put too low to avoid a sense of hopelessness in reaching them, in which event the shortfall is understated. Hedrick Smith observes:

> ... the Plan mentality has ... spawned a chaos all its own. Because the Plan, and ultimately that means the Kremlin leadership operating through Gosplan [the state planning agency] has demanded more than can reasonably be delivered by an economy of chronic shortages, the Plan has engendered storming [crash programmes], feather-bedding in factory work-forces, the end-of-the-month hassle over raw materials, the shortchanging, phoney figures, and systematic deception at all levels.

Let not the socialist loyalist believe that all this happens only in the USSR. It recurs, in a lesser or larger degree, in all state-run systems, even in the caring, benign British National Health Service. A USSR scientific institute found near the end of a year that it had not fully spent

its fund for new equipment: it promptly bought an expensive but unnecessary gadget rather than risk a cutback in its following yearly allocation. And that is precisely what happens in the National Health Service. Socialism—'if the taxpayer pays, who cares?'—is essentially the same everywhere. Don't blame the Russian scientist or the British hospital administrator. Blame socialism.

(7) Individual freedom, liberty, coercion

I repeat my argument, made above under (4), that there is less freedom in socialism and that it is more difficult to maintain than under capitalism. But the fundamental reason is essential in understanding the difference between socialism and capitalism.

I have argued that socialism sometimes has to relax its centralised controls and allow decentralisation in order to stimulate individual effort and output. But this policy has dangers. The taste of liberty in having more say in local factory management and decisions in production stimulates the taste for other liberties. The decisive dilemma is whether it stimulates irrepressible desire for civil, social, cultural and political freedom. That is the Polish, the Hungarian, the Russian dilemma; it would also be the British dilemma.

So far, the socialist regimes have put the preservation of their political power before the prospects of stimulating economic production. That is why, at least so far, liberty is much more precarious under socialism. And here I agree with the BBC's correspondent in the USSR from 1974 to 1976 and in China from 1977 to 1981 on the differences between them on the prospects for liberty:

> In both China and the Soviet Union, the fate of political reform has been inseparable from the reform of the economic system. Teng [Hsiao-ping] wanted more political democracy, because without it economic modernisation could not succeed. Khrushchev and Brezhnev refused to liberalise the Soviet economy *because they feared the political consequences it would entail.** (*My italics.*)

But in the long run even Soviet socialism will be unable to resist the longing for personal liberty that the occasional bouts of economic decen-

* *Philip Short, The Dragon and The Bear: Inside China and Russia Today*, Hodder and Stoughton, 1982.

tralisation will unintentionally arouse and strengthen. And that is why I differ from Hedrick Smith's conclusion in his otherwise deeply incisive study of *The Russians*. He faithfully describes the almost indescribable chaos, injustices, corruption and privations, but ends by doubting whether the Russians will want to change under their new tormentors. He quotes his wife, who accompanied him on his stay in Russia:

> . . . it's nothing new. It was the same under the Czars. They're the same people.

But they are not. In the sixty-five years since the Tsars the new technical marvels have told the Russians of the lives they and their children *could* lead under freedom—under capitalism, even perhaps under the market socialism that Professor Nove seems to think is 'feasible'. They will not accept the widening gulf between socialist servitude and Western liberty: not even if it requires civil war.

(8) Efficiency/inefficiency

An economic system is efficient if it produces what people want as *consumers*, not what they think is convenient to produce as *producers* (nor what politicians think they should want as consumers). Consumers are not always well-informed, resistant to advertisers' persuasion or all-wise. But an economic system based on the assumptions that they must therefore be spoonfed by 'experts' or benevolent despots is even worse than a system that tries to discover what consumers want. For a paternalistic or autocratic system, such as socialism at its best or worst, is even more objectionable. It ends with the consumer as the 'residuary legatee', who must take whatever the system produces, which is decided by politicians pressurised by producer interests. Whatever the familiar promises of socialism that it will be a 'people's democracy', in which the politicians will faithfully make the system work, in the real world it fails to produce one example in which the consumer is king. In practice he is the tame dog wagged by the political, bureaucratic or producer tail.

The 'planners' do not know, are not even anxious to discover, what the people want: without markets they have no efficient way of finding out. The people cannot require the planners to serve them. The planners, at best, guess what the people want, or should have, or will tolerate, and produce accordingly, whether this be food, clothing, housing or the increasing comforts of the ordinary people in capitalist countries. More often than not, the people in socialist countries get what the producers produce, and, if this is not to their liking—too bad. What else can they do? They can escape into black markets, and they do. They can try bribery, and if they have the money, they do. They can try blackmail, or threats, and if they have political influence, they do. But they cannot escape to the outside, capitalist, world from which their leaders have 'saved' them.

All these inefficiences—and worse—recur in different forms wherever the state concentrates power, whether in the Soviet Union or the British National Health Service.

(9) Monopoly

'Monopoly capitalism' has long been a socialist red bull, a rallying cry to the faithful. But what did the socialists do? They replaced private monopoly by state monopoly—deceptively described by euphemisms like 'nationalised industries', 'public enterprise', 'public corporations'.

State monopoly *may* be a regrettable necessity or an unnecessary evil if the goods or services can be produced in no other way—the public goods (another euphemism, implying that all other 'goods' are not public, or less public). Western government—not least in Britain—has spread itself far beyond public goods. Yet state *monopoly* is not unavoidable in fuel or transport, steel or telecommunications, education or medicine. Nor is local government monopoly unavoidable in most of the services it supplies.

And has 'public' monopoly demonstrated advantages that persuade us to continue it where it is not unavoidable? Are British consumers satisfied they are better served by British Rail, or the National Coal Board, or state education, or the National Health Service, or local refuse collection or local libraries than if they had a choice of suppliers? No British government until the first Thatcher government even asked the question. Do British workers feel less alienated from the political–administrative hierarchy in coal, steel, the railways, than they would be from private employers? Do taxpayers think they are getting better value for money? Do British citizens as voters think they have more say in, or control over, these organisations because they are called 'public services' or are the nominal 'owners' of infinitesimal particles?

Socialism is still sold politically—as the 'caring' society *par*

excellence because people 'care' for what they own in common. State monopoly ownership of the 'basic industries' or 'commanding heights' is as good a label in political advertising as any of the 'caring' slogans. But the tragic—and rather ugly—truth is that the more common ownership there is, the *less* the 'caring'. What is owned by everyone is, in effect, owned by no-one: each British citizen owns one fifty-five millionth of every train, coal-pit (including those that produce more stone than coal), outdated steel mill, vandalised post box, neglected school, dilapidated hospital, refuse-removal van, library, and hundreds and thousands of other items shared in common. How much 'care' does each citizen feel he should take of it? What do we do if we see them obviously uncared for? Mobilise an army of amateur caretakers? Or steal away hoping 'they' will do something? The sad lesson of socialism is that if the taxpayer (that is, someone else, or everyone in general) pays, who the hell cares?

(10) Corruption

Corruption is practised in capitalism: the social hospitality, the unasked-for favour, the Christmas gift. But it is infinitesimal compared with corruption in socialism.

The USSR must be taken as the best-documented example, although Philip Short has now recorded substantially similar developments in China. 'Practical' men are sometimes scornful of 'theory'; but every strategy of action, in industry, or government, or war, is based on a probable explanation or 'theory' of what consequences will follow from what activity. It is easy to explain why corruption could be expected to develop more easily in socialism than in capitalism. The theory is simply that corruption is a substitute for the free market, in which people exchange goods and services against money, or against each other, because under socialism nearly every shortage can be alleviated by offering a private reward, and people are prepared to risk detection and imprisonment.

And so it is not surprising to find widespread corruption in the USSR. Hedrick Smith in *The Russians*, Philip Short in *The Dragon and the Bear* and Konstantin Simis in *USSR: Secrets of a Corrupt Society* testify to the prevalence of a practice that socialists would have expected to be cleansed by the sense of community and moral teaching of socialism.

This evidence cannot all be accepted at its face value. Simis specialised in comparative law at the Institute of Soviet Legislation—in the Ministry of Justice—from 1966 to 1977. In 1976 the KGB raided his home and found the manuscript. But the first draft had been smuggled over to the West and he was fired. When his wife, also a lawyer, agreed to represent Anatoly Shcharansky, she was debarred. The KGB threatened to send Simis to a labour camp unless he and his wife left the USSR. They flew to Vienna in November 1977, and now live in Virginia.

His book shows a country suffused with corruption in almost every department of economic life—not only in the familiar daily goods and services but also housing, education and health, and not least but most debilitating, the police, justice and in government itself. Its saving grace for socialists is that soviet socialism would grind to a halt without it. It could also justify the description of the USSR as the Reluctant Soviet Market Economy.

The final irony is that corruption—or the free market, tolerated or suppressed—is so widespread in soviet socialism, where even savage penalties of large fines and uncomfortable imprisonment cannot suppress it, that it is increasingly tolerated, largely because it is irrepressible—and may be beneficial! There are the two standards reported by Vladimir Bukovsky: that people act differently in private from the way in which they speak in public—a form of degrading self-mockery that betrays the high ideals of socialism. The wheel has turned full circle. Socialism cannot suppress capitalism: capitalism has come to the rescue of the socialism that Marx said would replace it. Corruption was common under the authoritarian Tsarist bureaucracy, and basically for much the same kind of reasons: that the Tsars also suppressed the spontaneous evolution of markets. But the attempt by the Soviets to suppress the impulse to private exchange of all kinds has given corruption a stimulus that may in the end help to destroy soviet socialism. For, although illegal in Soviet law, it represents in one form the revolt of the masses against overgovernment. Again the Austrian economist Böhm-Bawerk will be vindicated: if the pen is mightier than the sword, the urge to truck and barter will prevail over the state.

So much for how socialism works in the real day-to-day world. But socialists find it difficult to accept that their gold can turn to dross. The former Professor Wlodzimierz Brus, dismissed as the Professor of Political Economy from the University of Warsaw and now a Fellow of Wolfson

College, Oxford, where he has been since 1973, is one of the increasing number of European socialist economists who have come to see the indispensability of markets, in socialism as well as in capitalism.

In an article (*Survey*, Autumn 1980) Dr Brus says it is now 'a non-controversial reflection in textbooks' that state action is essential under any economic system 'for five' purposes:

(1) To control monopoly;
(2) To deal with ('internalise') externalities;
(3) To offset the short-time horizons of markets;
(4) To lessen uncertainties;
(5) To dampen fluctuations.

He maintains the Marxist interpretation of the tendency to increasing state control for these purposes—the internal contradictions of the capitalist system in which the development of productive forces is 'increasingly hampered by the nature of production relations based on private ownership'. This, he says, explains 'the continuing pressure for broadening the scope and criteria for appropriation and action'. Even if this Marxist gobblydygook were crystal clear to the British people, where is *their* 'continuing pressure' for (presumably state) 'appropriation and action'?

In any event, none of these supposed reasons for 'state action' constitutes a case or strengthens the argument for socialism. Not only are some of them worse and more difficult, as argued in this chapter, to remove in socialism. Dr Brus, like many market socialists, overlooks the inherent abuses of socialism (Chapter 3). After sixty years of experience of socialism in one form or another in Europe and other countries, it cannot still be supposed that government is equipped to right the wrongs that socialists identify in capitalism. Or is this one more manifestation of the socialist's fear of discovering that, after all, socialism is as unreal as a dream?

5

After a Hundred Years:
Time to Bury Socialism

What has socialism accomplished after a hundred years of proselytising, preaching, insurrection and civil war since the death of Marx in 1883?

Whatever may be claimed for other parts of his speculations, his economics have been an almighty flop. He found fault with capitalism but had almost no notion of how the socialism that was to replace it would work. And he certainly had little understanding of the role of markets in assessing the mass of information required by the central planners.

Many, if not most, socialist economists in Europe have long accepted that socialism cannot dispense with markets. British economists seem the main exception. They do not show knowledge of the work of Durbin, Dickinson, Dobb, Lerner and other British economists who, fifty years ago, were forced to recognise the impossibility of socialism—or any economic system—that dispensed entirely with markets.

The opposition of socialists to markets is itself something of a mystery. There was nothing in the writings of Lenin that saw markets as the work of the capitalist devil. Indeed, he had the good sense to restore them only three years after 1917. Writing 'as a theorist reared in Marxism (an offshoot, it must be remembered, of the classical school of economists)', Raymond Fletcher, a Labour MP for fifteen years for a mining constituency, has said, 'Neither Marx, Engels nor Lenin ever prepared a detailed blueprint for the kind of society they expected would be created by the victorious proletariat; but there is nothing in their texts to support the view that the abolition of economic and social inequality must involve the abolition of the market as a means of pricing and allocating scarce resources'. When the Austrian economist, Ludwig von Mises, argued in 1921 that socialism would founder without markets because it

49

could not calculate the value of resources, especially capital, he was derided by socialist economists in Britain—and still is by some today.

Imports and exports interfere with the best-laid plans of even socialist mice and men to plan a socialist country from the centre. Socialism in one country is at least conceivable (though I do not agree with Professor Nove* that it is 'feasible'—unless it is small, with a simple economic structure); but socialism in a *world* (or even a continent like Europe) of free-trading countries, socialist or capitalist, is a planners' nightmare. That is why logical British socialists want to abandon the Common Market, so that they can isolate and socialise at least Britain on its own. And it also explains why more megalomanic British socialists think on a bigger scale that, by staying in the Common Market and drawing in even more European countries, they can make the whole of Europe socialist.

The nightmare of planning very large areas from the centre was foreseen by socialist theoreticians from the early days. Marx promised a book on how to solve the conundrum; perhaps it is just as well he did not write it because it would have shown him to be even more of a tyro on the day-to-day working of socialism. Karl Kautsky, an early socialist thinker, saw the dilemma, but proposed the wrong solution: 'a degree of self-sufficiency and autarchy'—that is, socialism would have to come first in one country, and in the rest of the world—socialist or capitalist—second. But this funk-hole did not satisfy Professor Nove, and he spurned it with a mighty intellectual wallop, again tinged with humour, although this time more astringent.

Since markets must play 'a major role' *within* socialism, he tried to explain, they must also do so *between* socialist countries. And that sets the doctrinal cat amongst the socialist pigeons. Since Lenin and earlier they have asserted that capitalism is the source of international conflict. Out now goes Lenin and all that stuff about war being caused by capitalist imperialism. Socialist states, Professor Nove now says clearly for the especial benefit of socialist simpletons, can, may or will also occasionally engage in a little conflict—over, say oil, So Kautsky's autarky (he did not forsee oil) is no solution. It implies either a world socialist commonwealth (directed, perhaps in rotation from, say, Havana, Nicaragua or Addis Ababa, since Moscow could not claim per-

* In his *Economics of Feasible Socialism, op. cit.*

manent sovereignty). Or it implies the Marxist dream of superabundance 'in which', mocks Professor Nove gently, 'the comrades in West Africa freely decide to supply cocoa and bananas in just the right quantities to the comrades in Western Europe for sheer love of humanity, without the requirement of any *quid pro quo*'. 'Not a very likely story, to put it mildly,' ends Professor Nove wearily, with perhaps a touch of outrage at having to explain it all yet again.

This ridicule tinged with humour may be the best way to end the hold that 'socialism' continues to exert on both the untutored mind, young or uninformed, secular or clerical, yearning for a society of brotherly love and for the sophisticated politician or academic who sees in the promises of dreams, technically impressive (like those of the British socialist economists (Chapter 3)) but wildly unrealistic, the prospect of power to run society in their socialist image. We may have taken socialism too seriously for too long. We have cowered before socialists as though they were intellectual giants, because of their outer defences of spiritual assertiveness.

But one socialist who has understood the argument very clearly, Peter Kellner, Political Editor of the *New Statesman*, wrote* that Professor Nove had argued:

> wholly convincingly that Marx's idea of socialism is absurd and always has been . . . Nove . . . argues that . . . any attempt to dismantle the mechanisms of the market lead inexorably to inefficient centralised planning, and to corrupt centralised power . . .

The early Russian socialists instinctively understood the role of the market. Trotsky said in 1922:

> It is necessary for each state-owned factory with its technical director, to be subject not only to control from the top . . . but also from below, by the market, which will remain the regulator of the state economy for a long time to come.

And Lenin reintroduced the market, after the chaos following its destruction in the 1917 Revolution. The market was again destroyed in 1928–9 not because it had failed to reinvigorate the Russian economy, but because Stalin, who replaced Lenin, found it an obstacle to the cen-

* *New Statesman*, 11 March 1983.

tralisation of political power under his control. This ulterior purpose was camouflaged by all kinds of economic arguments, some echoed by Brus (Chapter 4), that the market was too slow to reach national objectives, such as rapid industrialisation. These objectives were laid down, of course, by Stalin, not by the people of Russia, although to placate the Western sympathisers with communism, Stalin produced in 1935 a new liberal constitution that fooled many British socialists, including some at the London School of Economics in my student days. But Stalin's more rapid technique that replaced the 'slow' market—liquidation of 10 million peasant farmers—is the alternative that present-day socialists would hardly say in public they still prefer.

Kellner's conclusion is that, in the centenary year of Marx's death, the British Labour Party must, at long last, undertake an agonising re-appraisal of the interrelationships between Marxism, socialism and British Labour. He says that the role of the market as essential in the *transition* to socialism is scarcely questioned on the British Left. I doubt that proposition: Healey, Shore and some trade union leaders like Chapple, a former communist who exposed corruption in his union, understand the market, but it seems unlikely that its function has ever been considered, still less understood, by Kinnock, Hattersley, Meacher and most other Labour leaders or contenders, least of all by trade union leaders like Basnett, General Secretary of the General and Municipal Works Union (GMWU). On the contrary, the market (or 'market forces') is seen as the enemy of the people and of socialism (the two are usually confused) by Kinnock, Benn, and trade union leaders like Gill, a communist leader in the Amalgamated Union of Engineering Workers (AUEW), and Bickerstaffe. But Kellner goes further, and here he must have sent shock-waves through the governing board as well as the editorial staff of the *New Statesman*. The market is not only a regrettable necessity on the way to socialism. He says Professor Nove envisages the market as 'a medium-to-long term positive objective' as part of a mixed socialist economy with state enterprises for 'basic' services like electricity, socialised enterprises responsible to their employers rather than primarily to the state (as in Yugoslavia), small-scale co-operative enterprises, small-scale *private* enterprises and self-employed workers, plumbers and what may be regarded as other personal capitalists, including, no doubt, journalists, playwrights and economists. Kellner concludes that, after a hundred years of Marxist influence on socialism and Labour party linking, 'it is time for Labour to bury Marx'.

Other sophisticated socialists, such as Leszek Kolakowski (below), conscious that something is radically wrong with the historical/traditional/conventional view of socialism as an economy run ultimately by the state, have been working on other solutions. Kellner's formula 'Labour without Marx' was preceded in 1978 by a troubled book by Evan Luard, a former Junior Labour Minister, whose solution is 'Labour without the State'. The recognition that a state-dominated economy will not yield the results that good men, including well-intentioned socialists, want is also seen in Michael (Lord) Young, another Labour intellectual (now SDP), who would dispense with the state, or severely discipline it, by an expansion of co-operation between individuals in the form of 'mutual aid', although he envisages also some activity in 'quasi-markets'.

My reply to all such socialist anxieties to remove the state wherever possible, which as a liberal I share, is that the only system in which there would be no arbitrary limits to local, voluntary, mutual, co-operative, provident activity (such as was growing in the nineteenth century provident and trade union insurance before the state, first in public utilities, communications, transport, fuel, and then welfare, suppressed it) is *an open society with free access to newcomers in economic activity of all kinds*. But that is the market economy from which socialist, even some SDP, thinkers fight shy. Let people do as much as they wish outside the market. But let them, or their intellectual mentors, socialist or mutualist, not close the market if *the people* find it more effective for some activities, services and economic activity.

So I have an even better proposal as a resolution for socialists who would like to be known as democrats, in the sense that they see socialism as serving the people not as manipulating the people to serve the socialist planners, officials, and others who run the socialist machine or who support it because they do well out of it. Kellner does not go far enough in demonstrating his explanation of Professor Nove's argument for 'feasible' socialism. The use of markets is not only a 'medium-to-long term objective'. Markets can eventually be dispensed with only when scarcity has been replaced by superabundance, so that there is no need to evaluate goods and services in exchange because there is no sacrifice in having enough of everything for everybody. The sacrifice is described by economists—after the Austrian Friedrich Wieser (1851–1926)—as 'opportunity cost', that is, the sacrifice (or 'loss') of B or C or D in having more of A. But Professor Nove's central critique of Marxist economy is that the supposition that superabundance will emerge to solve all 'economic' problems of choosing between alternatives to minimise the sacrifice is not a *solution* to the economic problem but a monumental *evasion* of it. It begs the whole question that economists have been busy for two centuries trying to solve. And here comes Marx thinking he has solved it in one book! For his assumption of the magical emergence of superabundance is Marxist, day-dreaming, Utopia. Professor Nove tries laboriously to persuade his fellow-socialists to see this unhappy conclusion in his long section, 'The Legacy of Marx', of over 30,000 words. The 'legacy', he concludes apocalyptically, is *nothing*: 'classical Marxism has no answer.' What a fall was there, my countrymen: as ever, Shakespeare put it better than anyone else.

Nove patiently quotes the American Marxist Charles Taylor, who questions: 'how we envisage men's situations to have changed, what constraints, divisions, tensions, dilemmas, struggles and estrangements will replace those we know today . . . Marxism implies the answer is "none": that our only situation will be that of generic man, harmoniously linked in contest with nature. But this predicament is not only unbelievable, but arguably unlivable.'* And that is the inescapable *impasse* now reached: superficially brilliant dialectics with no solutions. Marxism has reached the end of its long, hard, cruel, blind alley. Taylor's *cri de coeur* should end socialist self-delusion, wishful thinking, the deceit of false hopes for all time. But it will not.

If Marx had no answers, why does Marxism linger? Peter Kellner approaches the answer. The powerful attraction of Marxism is that it holds out the promise of superabundance, in which jealousies, envies, covetousness, theft, cheating and all human vices will have been made superfluous. There will then be free, unpriced, distribution of the good things in life 'to each according to his needs'. Marx said this in 1875; Kellner says he borrowed/stole it from Bakunin and a group of anarchists in the 1871 Paris commune. A correspondent to the *New Statesman* claimed that Bakunin borrowed it from the French Utopian communist, Louis Blanc in the 1840s. My guess is that it was taken from the early millennarians.

But 'free goods' is not an intellectual attraction; it is based on no plausible, logical demonstration that sometime, somewhere, the supply of everything will magically outrun the demand. Lenin in 1919 (*State and*

* C. Taylor, *Hegel and Modern Society*, Cambridge University Press, 1979.

Revolution) tried to explain the transition of this first or lower phase of communism in which distribution was according to *work* (because there was still scarcity and therefore inducements to people to give their best) to the second or higher phase in which distribution was according to *need* because scarcity had been abolished and no-one minded who received how much. But Lenin argued that the transition also required a change in human nature, so that no-one would mind who received how much. Since then there has been endless argument over the chicken and the egg: which comes first? Does abundance make men selfless? or does selflessness create abundance? Only one side can win this argument.

So, as Kellner says, the attraction of a world of abundance must lie elsewhere. He says the solution is not intellectual but moral. It is not clear what he means by moral, except that it is something *not* based on reasoned argument, logic and evidence. And that is the essence of the whole argument against the feasibility of socialism. The Marxist vision of superabundance is that of the child dreaming that everything is made of sugar and spice, of the chase after rainbows, the gambler who sees himself winning the pools, the eternal optimist, the visionary, the phantasist. Professor Norman Cohn, the former University of Sussex historian, has filled a long book on the millennarians discussing their numerous ways to escape from everyday, sub-optimal, decision-enforcing life. And Melvin Lasky (editor of *Encounter*) had an equally long book, *Utopia and Revolution* (1976) which complements it. Even with technical marvels yet unknown, all we can say is that *supply* will grow unprecedentedly; we can say nothing about *demand*. Some goods or services will become so plentiful and cheap that distribution can be almost free (but not water, if I may correct Professor Nove, which is not superabundant, requires costly equipment to purify and distribute, and should indeed not be regarded as free, but be *charged* for to encourage economy and conservation). But goods in general will remain scarce relatively to demand. So they will entail opportunity costs. And there will have to be continuing refinement of the methods studied by economists to minimise the opportunity cost—the loss of sacrifice of, say, a margin of clothing, food, drink, or motoring—when an individual wants more housing. And that means markets will continue to be essential for a long time to yield their unique, indispensable information on opportunity costs. And socialism will not serve mankind *for as far ahead as we can see*.

The prospect of abolishing scarcity—the dawn of abundance to end struggle, strife, sacrifice, costs: the advent of a world of plenty with no more poverty, want, hunger, hardship, involuntary unemployment, and all the miseries we had just suffered in the 1929–31 Great Depression so overwhelmed my young mind in 1936 that I wrote to John Strachey. He had described in his stream of Left Book Club titles—*The Nature of Capitalist Crisis*, *The Coming Struggle for Power*, and the others—the appealing prospect that would welcome mankind when crumbling capitalism finally crumbled. (Strachey said Hitler had brought capitalism to its final phase in fascist Germany—another tragic inversion of the truth, which was that Hitler had in the event 'used' the German capitalists to establish national socialism, not the capitalists who had used him to destroy communism.) Socialist Left Book Club teaching was that, when capitalism was at last replaced by communism, it would promptly abolish scarcity. What a delightful prospect! How long, I asked, did Strachey think the delicious process would take? Seventy-five years, he replied. I wonder, if he were living today, and looked around the world as it is, whether he would be more regretful of the false hopes with which he had fed students than are the other false prophets of the 1930s. But at least we can say of them and their friends at the LSE that they weakened our intellectual resistance to socialist communism rather than actively strengthened communism, as did their opposite numbers in Cambridge.

So abundance will elude mankind for as long ahead as we can see. And Marxist socialism *without* markets has no solution for mankind. So far Nove (and Kellner)—and other socialists like Kolakowski, the Polish historian expelled from Warsaw University, later at Oxford, mostly those who have seen post-war socialism at first hand in Europe, though not the British socialist economists at Cambridge or Sussex (where Stuart Holland, the left-wing Labour MP, taught from 1971 to 1979). The key question is therefore: Can socialism work *with* markets? For this is the only form of socialism that can offer some prospect of tolerable living standards, some progress, and a degree of individual liberty. But for reasons discussed earlier, my answer has to be *No*.

The reason, to repeat it in a sentence, is that markets in socialism will be used or tolerated only as long as they suit the *political* controllers, whereas for markets to give their maximum benefit to the people they must operate wherever it is for their good, *whether or not it suits the political controllers*. And since the power of government—autocratic or representative—to control or suppress markets is least under capitalism,

HOW MANIFESTOS ARE WORKED OUT···

"Just putting on a touch of Socialism···

A little more won't do any harm···

May as well finish the job while we're about it ···

And we'd better "make it irreversible!

especially the minimal-government capitalism liberals favour, and the power of government is more dangerous, arbitrary and autocratic in socialism, socialists who now understand that markets are indispensable *must abandon their socialism.*

Indeed, since markets are not only desirable, but irrepressible, the days of politically enforced socialism are, in any event, numbered. It is easier to suppress them in the peasant cultures of Russia than in the Western cultures of Hungary and Poland. There will come a time—even in Russia—when the urgency of restoring sagging socialist production will persuade the political controllers to allow, or shut a blind eye to, industrial decentralisation that will create economic freedoms too extensive to suppress the desire to accompany them by civil, political, cultural freedom. Where many trade among themselves, buy and sell farm produce, clothes, furnishings, house equipment . . . Why, they will ask, may we not also write and exchange our thoughts among ourselves, teach what we think is right, listen to scholars, meet to discuss our problems and the ways ahead? Then it will be too late to stop the economic market from engendering the latent, long-suppressed desire for civil liberties. Then the fat will be in the fire. Then the attempt of the regime to suppress the incipient urge to liberty will go further than in Poland. Then the brittle egg of socialism will crack and disintegrate. Then the expropriators of liberty will be expropriated by their victims.

The further proposal I would add to Kellner's, that Labour should abandon Marx, is therefore that, if Labour wishes to serve its people, intead of creating a haven for political activists, technocrats and bureaucrats *it must abandon socialism.* It must now, as other comparable Left-inclined parties, formerly stained by socialism, in Australia, Canada, West Germany and other countries in Europe, abandon not only a hundred years of Marx, but also sixty years of Clause IV that contemplated the nationalisation of production, distribution and exchange.

Labour could then join the rest of the political and academic community in discovering new ways of creating a market-based economy and open, voluntary, co-operative society, with state economy only where essential, but elsewhere private enterprise and endeavour—commercial, voluntary, provident or mutual. Otherwise I see a widening gulf between the Labour leaders—who cannot recognise the lessons of socialism—and their remaining working-class but increasingly embourgeoised rank and file who will no longer see socialist Labour as its natural champion and will move to the SDP, the Liberals or to the new

Thatcher Conservatives who have shown themselves more sensitive to working-class aspirations.

That would leave socialist Labour leaders with perhaps 10–15 per cent of the rank and file, comprising the old Labour supporters aged sixty-five and over or the younger idealists still seduced by socialist promises in the Marxist mirage of superabundance. Labour will retain a dwindling proportion of its industrial parliamentary seats in the 1987–8 and 1991–2 general elections until it virtually loses its status as a Parliamentary power by the end of the century.

But Professor Nove does not demonstrate *how* the market can be absorbed into socialist economy, nor in particular, *how the political controllers can be expected to allow the market to work when it conflicts with their political control.*

Nove deals with how markets *should* be integrated into socialism, but his thought is filled with general hopes and aspirations rather than with effective incentives to success and sanctions for failure. Yet this is the essential task that market capitalism, in spite of its faults, has *solved*. Nove's discussion on how a market-based economy would work begins with the sad confession that Rosa Luxemburg had no idea. The early warnings of Enrico Barone about the chaos that would engulf socialism if it did not use markets, says Nove, 'fell on deaf ears'. The Russian economist Kautsky in 1910 simply regurgitated the vague notions of Marx and Engels and envisaged socialism as a single gigantic (capitalist?) firm directed from the centre. He anticipated Trotsky and Bukharin in sensing that workers could not be allowed to work where they wished. Not until Oskar Lange, the Polish economist, educated in the West, who did understand the necessity for markets, did socialist economists after the Second World War resume the task of showing how the centre could inform itself of the demands at the circumference. But his over-confident solution—speed-of-light computers—was a feeble substitute for the real market.

This whole debate between economists on whether relevant calculation is feasible under socialism, which started with Mises in 1921 (or in an earlier form by warnings of the Italian economist Enrico Barone in 1907) and flared up in the 1930s, was recently summed up by Hayek, a student of Mises', in the April 1982 *Journal of Economic Affairs* (which appeared after Nove completed his book). Hayek dismissed the notion of calculation by socialist 'markets' in a few lines:

> It is 'pure fiction' to suppose that information required by each of millions of producers can be aggregated by the planning authority. It may assemble information about *quantities* but each [capitalistic] producer knows *values* (based on scarcities). The capitalist market enables individual producers to adapt their activities to a multitude of circumstances which in their totality are *not known to anyone*. (*My italics*.)

Economics has yet to explain this process. For socialism to claim to have solved it is pretentious; it simply cannot assemble the required information. Without real open market prices, the opportunity costs cannot be known.

And a young Polish economist at Oxford argued, also in the *Journal of Economic Affairs* (July 1982), that socialist calculation had been shown by Mises (in 1949, *Human Action*, replying to Lange) to be impossible not only in practice but also in theory. Even if all the required information (on *value*, not only quantity) could be conveyed, perhaps by speed-of-light computer, to the planning authority, it could not be used because *the economic system was in a constant state of change and the information would be out of date before it could be transmitted and production 'plans' changed*.

Nove does not solve the market socialists' dilemma; he outlines only general principles on how market socialism *should* work. And his attempt to reconcile consumer and producer interests does not show clearly which must take precedence in the event of a conflict of interests. 'How should production be organised?' he says. 'What *categories of producers* of goods and services should exist? What forms of property in means of production?' Questions, but no answers.

'Several ideas come together here. The first is the need for variety, and for opportunities for individual and group initiative. We must bear in mind the need to avoid or minimise the feeling of alienation, and take into account *producers' preferences* . . .' [Nove's italics]. This is a very vague and dangerous formulation: *consumers*' preferences must *predominate*, otherwise men as producers will take shortsighted views about their jobs, security, pay, conditions of work, overpay themselves, eat into capital, and sacrifice their own long-term interests.

'While consumer preferences, user needs, should certainly predominate [meaning prevail?] in determining what to produce, the preference of the work force should play a major role [how much is that?] in determining how it should be produced, bearing in mind the need for economy of resources and the technology available. Of course, "how" and "what" can overlap. Thus railwaymen may prefer not to run a late-night train to the detriment of suburban theatre-goers, and one then needs to reconcile conflicting interests.'

And much more in the same vein. Nove may have taught socialists that socialism must use markets, but they cannot use the outdated information it might assemble (in quantities). Capitalism is sixty years or more ahead of socialism in how to use the real market, in which local information is used by individual entrepreneurs on the spot, *and* are rewarded if they use it efficiently and penalised if they use it inefficiently. Socialism fails precisely because it does not do that, or if it tried would provoke civil war.

I cannot therefore see why Nove remains a socialist. That revelation also applies to other market socialists—Ota Sik of Czechoslavakia (now teaching in Switzerland), Brus, the Polish economist (now at Oxford), Kornai of Hungary (now in Budapest), Kolakowski (also at Oxford) and others.

But I am not surprised at the continuing conservatism of British political socialist leaders like Eric Heffer, or academics such as Ralph Miliband, Professor Eric Hobsbawm or E. P. Thompson, and activists excited by the sound of battle against the omnibus enemy 'capitalism', exemplified in the brighter new *Marxism Today*, the 'theoretical and discussion' journal of the Communist Party. They are elated more by the intellectual hunt than by the policy 'kill', and are more interested in refining their theories than in applying them in the real imperfect world with imperfect people achieving results, even if imperfect. But they are professional chasers after holy grails; they can exert their preferences in a free market capitalist society, but they would not be allowed to 'drop out' in the fully centralised socialist society for which they yearn. They will not care if they lose their rank and file in the long and uncertain quest for Utopia, in which the economic problem is 'solved' simply by being assumed to have been swamped by superabundance. This is the problem that capitalism is still grappling with, and making continuous if not uninterrupted progress in solving. That is why socialism will lose—or has lost—its magical appeal, and why the rank and file will turn to capitalism for higher living standards and personal liberty.

Socialism offers the mass of people nothing unless it is more likely than capitalism to abolish scarcity. Nothing in the theory or practice of socialism suggests that it would. The theory is non-existent on the abolition of scarcity. But the practice is clear: wherever in the world you can go some way to compare socialism with capitalism because their cultural backgrounds are similar you find, on the contrary, that it is capitalism that has gone furthest in mastering scarcity by raising living standards: West and East Germany, South and North Korea, Switzerland and Austria, Singapore and Sri Lanka, Japan and India, Taiwan and mainland China, Hong Kong and Shanghai. And even within the socialist–communist world, the countries that are dealing better with scarcity are those making use of markets and decentralisation: no wonder Andropov (and Honecker of East Germany and Jaruzelski of Poland) cast envious eyes at Hungary and Yugoslavia, but dare not copy them for fear of risking political power.

and, as the Brandt–Heath Commission will discover, in the South as well as the North—want results—*performance*. They can choose perfect but impossible socialism, or imperfect but feasible capitalism. Where the people are allowed to choose they choose capitalism—even where they elect 'socialist' governments for a term which they know cannot do much harm because they would be restrained or ejected if they tried to introduce socialism: France, Spain, Greece, even Sweden.

Envoi

British socialism (or European, or African, or Asian, or South American) has had a lot to say in condemnation of capitalism, and some of it was justified (except the argument that its faults were ineradicable—Chapter 3).

But that was only half the task of socialism. The other half was to put something better in the place of capitalism—less inefficient, less inhumane, more just, less wasteful, more respectful of human dignity.

But what *better* has it put in its place? The tragic, blunt, undeniable, astonishing, appalling, truth is—*NOTHING*. It has excelled capitalism in none of these aspects.

Socialism had a case: capitalism was imperfect: it is, and so remains. Socialism, therefore, proceeded to undermine it, and the process committed the ultimate crime against humanity. Socialism

> destroyed half a loaf and replaced it with less;
> promised brotherly love, but provoked civil war;
> promised plenty, but destroyed the seedcorn;
> promised liberty, but has created slavery;
> promised equality, but produced inescapable hierarchy.

Now in the 1980s it still has a case against imperfect capitalism. But from the newest forms of Marxism to the latest compromises of the Labour National Executive Committee it offers no more than its familiar assortment of conjecture, surmise, plans, intentions, promises, pie-in-the-sky, wills-o'-the-wisp, jam tomorrow, promises of eternal brotherhood, promises of plenty, promises of new concordats between trade union leaders (not rank and file) and the Labour NEC, promises, promises, promises, dreams of perfection, dreams of selflessness, promises . . .

A century of dreams and promises is enough.

It is time to return to reality to make what we can of imperfect man and the imperfect institutions he has evolved to make the best of nature's niggardly resources.

It is time to resume the process of refining imperfect institutions to serve imperfect mankind.

Let those who dislike using their talents to make goods or services others want, exchanging for other goods or services, or for money in markets, to take care of their family, save for a rainy day, or give their money to good causes, drop out to form communes in which they abandon family life for communal sharing and mutual aid. No-one will stop them, so long as they are self-supporting. But let the rest of us get on with the business of living—working, exchanging, caring for families, giving where we wish. The demand of socialists that socialism be forced on people who don't want it has become obscene.

Socialism is a desirable Utopia but useless as a precept for living in the world we know. It 'solves' all the tasks and problems of human life by assuming them away. It offers no guidance to mankind trying to make the best of the world he has inherited. It offers only cul-de-sacs, blind alleys, mirages in the desert, dreams that turn to nightmares.

We have spent a century on a wild goose chase to a socialist nowhere. It has distracted and diverted us from the only task that is likely to be fruitful—working out the rules and principles of the economic system that encourages people to make the best of their talents and the resources under their management. Until the rules are perfected, the system will give very imperfect results—imperfect compared with the Utopia conjured up by the visionaries who shirk the task of improving the world as it is, but steadily less imperfect as the rules are refined and the principles clarified.

The only system that offers any prospect of this approach to perfection is the system that socialists have scorned and denounced without putting anything better in its place. They deride it as 'capitalism'. It is the system which decentralises power to people who stand to gain (or lose) if they use their resources wisely (or foolishly) based on the information they collect from consumer markets. It is a very imperfect system, but we had better return from whoring after false socialist gods to the task of perfecting it. It is all we have. The best hope of making it serve mankind better is to close the fairy-tale of socialism and return to the real world.

PART TWO

Everywhere a Failure

Brian Crozier

Prologue: The Universal Rules of Socialism

The first Universal Rule of socialism is that it fails wherever it is tried. It doesn't matter whether it calls itself Burmese socialism or African, whether the experiment takes place in Sweden or Tanzania or Cuba, it simply doesn't work.

The second Universal Rule is that the degree of failure is proportionate with the degree of socialism: the more there is of it, the worse the failure—allowing for other factors such as the stage of development reached before the experiment began and the aptitude for economic development of the nations and peoples concerned in the light of history, civilisation, culture, climate and any other relevant factor.

I hope in this second part of our study to demonstrate the truth of my two Universal Rules.

There is, however, a third Universal Rule, no less important than the other two: socialism is incompatible with freedom. Here again, the degree to which socialism has been adopted or imposed is crucial. Anybody who doubts my third Universal Rule is invited to look at the plight of the people in the most extreme socialist regimes in the world, which are probably those of the Chinese People's Republic, North Korea and Vietnam. In all three, individual freedom has been virtually extinguished.

This was particularly true of China under Mao Tse-tung, although the myth of Mao as a great and far-sighted leader was uncritically swallowed by many well-meaning people who would not have relished living under the tyranny he had established by force in his vast and ancient country. In all three of these Far Eastern 'models' of socialism, you cannot marry a person of your choice (as a Chinese girl discovered in the post-Mao

67

THE DUSTBIN OF HISTORY

Cummings

period when she made the mistake of falling in love with a French diplomat). Nor can you change your job at will: the all-pervasive Party tells you where to work, and in China, in particular, the Party might decide that it would do an intellectual good to work in the fields in a distant province.

In such countries, you cannot travel freely, either in the country or abroad. In North Korea, the Soviet-invented device of the 'internal passport' has become a thick book with a detailed family history back to the grandparents as a record of just about everything you have done and said in your life to date. As for travel abroad, only official visits are sanctioned, and then only in groups closely supervised by the secret police. As for emigrating, you do have the option of joining others in a leaky boat and risking your life on the high seas, as with the Vietnamese 'boat people'.

As for political rights, they are non-existent. Both China and Vietnam once experimented briefly with carefully metered political freedom in the 1950s. As Mao put it, 'Let one hundred flowers bloom, let one hundred schools of thought contend'. The North Vietnamese (as they then were) did much the same. In both countries, the degree of dissent revealed was so startling to the regimes that the lid was promptly clamped down again. Then after Mao Tse-tung had died, and the relatively pragmatic Teng Hsiao-ping had taken over, ordinary (that is, non-Party) people were allowed to write their opinions on a long slab of bricks in Peking known as 'Democracy Wall'. That, too, was a short-lived diversion.

But surely, some readers may say, you are talking about *communist*, not socialist, regimes. Shouldn't a distinction be made between the two?

The short answer to this legitimate query is that, again, it is all a question of degree. All communist regimes are totalist in that the ruling Communist Party (whether or not it uses the word 'Communist' in its designation: some do not) controls every aspect of people's lives, non-political as well as political. But not one of them, including the prototype model of all in the Soviet Union, claims to have achieved 'communism'. The promise of 'communism', seen as the advent of abundance for all, is like a mirage, ever receding into the distance, always in the future. The most these regimes claim is that they have achieved 'socialism', or that they are 'building' it. The Soviets claim to have *built* it, and to be pushing on towards communism, to be achieved at some unspecified date in the (far) future.

Indeed, the Soviets refer to their East European empire (which is what it is) as the 'Socialist Commonwealth'; not, say, as the 'communist bloc'. To describe the existing communist regimes as 'socialist' is thus merely to take them at their own valuation. The point is that socialism has been taken further in the communist countries than elsewhere, and it must be assumed that this is because it takes a totalist, one-party state to impose full socialism. Which merely illustrates the proposition that socialism extinguishes freedom.

In party democracies, where political parties may alternate in power or need to form coalitions to survive in office, there is at least a glimmer of hope, in that a new coalition or the advent of an anti-socialist party to power, may be given a chance to undo some, at least, of the harm done by the previous government's socialist programme.

Even in party democracies, however, the advance of socialism can be insidious, to the point where it is hard to reverse. As a well-known French political commentator puts it, 'Socialism is communism in homoeopathic doses.' In recent years Britain's Labour Party has called for 'a fundamental and irreversible shift in the balance of power and wealth in favour of working people and their families'. If this aim is ever achieved—that is, if 'irreversible' socialism is introduced—then indeed the liberties of the British people will have been extinguished.

In Western countries, until very recently, incoming non-socialist governments have been content on the whole to administer the situation they have inherited, whatever the degree of socialism their predecessors may have introduced. To that extent the march of socialism has tended to be 'irreversible'. In 1979 and 1980, however, two Western leaders committed to reversing the irreversible were elected to high office: Mrs Margaret Thatcher and President Ronald Reagan. Each has aimed at reducing the state's share of the national cake. In other words, at reducing the degree of socialism achieved by outgoing administrations. It is too early to judge to what extent these efforts will prove successful. That they are necessary and deserve full support, I do not doubt. In Britain, especially, the inroads of socialism had seriously undermined the freedom of the individual in recent years.

The case of Swedish socialism is of particular interest, and I shall give it close attention later on. Unlike other socialist-inclined countries, the emphasis in Sweden has not been on the nationalisation (or socialisation) of the means of production, distribution and exchange (to quote from the notorious Clause IV of the Constitution of Britain's Labour

Party). By and large, industry has been left in private hands, to create wealth which the state can then expropriate in the furtherance of socialism. (The party that has ruled Sweden for all but six years during the past five decades calls itself Social Democratic, but its leader, Olof Palme, is ideologically closer to the Soviets than to the Americans.)

The accumulated outcome of socialist policies in Sweden has been a regime which has the outer trappings of democracy—political parties, an elected parliament, a theoretically free press—but in which the prevailing socialist consensus has so far reduced individual freedom as to cause a British writer (Roland Huntford, who served in Stockholm as correspondent of the London *Observer*) to describe the Swedes as 'The New Totalitarians' (the title of the book he wrote about socialist Sweden). Once again, socialism and freedom are shown to be incompatible.

It may seem surprising that I have made only passing reference, so far, to the Union of Soviet Socialist Republics. Its turn, however, comes very soon. As the longest continuous experiment in socialism (1917 to 1983, so far), the Soviet Union is clearly of the utmost importance. At this stage, though, I want only to point to a paradox.

The Soviet Union is one of the most repressive regimes in the world, but it is *less totalist* than the regimes of China, North Korea and Vietnam in that it is marginally but significantly easier for ordinary people to opt out of the political process in the USSR than in the three Far Eastern socialist regimes. In China, for instance, every street, every small village has its Party committee, bullying or cajoling ordinary people to do the Party's bidding. In the USSR, no dissent is tolerated, but the Party is less all-pervasive. Corruption is rampant and the black market is a way of life: indeed it is hardly an exaggeration to say that it keeps the economic system alive, by preventing it from choking on the socialism of centralised planning. True, those on the fiddle, who perform a useful function, put themselves permanently at risk. Some 'economic crimes' are punishable by death. But to the extent that the fiddlers and black marketeers defeat the paralysis inherent in socialism, they contribute a tiny ray of freedom in the surrounding blackness.

6

The Soviet Prototype

It is not enough to assert that socialism has 'failed' in the Soviet Union. One must also offer criteria upon which to judge success or failure, and the best criteria are surely those advanced by the revolutionaries who seized power in Russia in November 1917, eight months after the popular upheaval which had swept away the regime of the Tsars.

It is, of course, difficult to separate the 'socialism' practised by the Soviet Communist Party (CPSU) from the ghastly crimes committed by that party, but I shall make the attempt. I am not writing about the crimes of Soviet communism but about the economic and social performance of socialism in a country in which the ruling party had unlimited power to impose and administer socialism.

What, then, did the Bolshevik revolutionaries of 1917 claim or promise they were going to do in Russia?

Lenin was, of course, the leader of the Bolshevik revolutionaries and he made his own contribution to socialist theory, but the essentials of Lenin's programme were, in fact, outlined nearly seventy years earlier by Karl Marx and Friedrich Engels in the Communist Manifesto. The Manifesto, published in 1848, called for state ownership of the land, banks, industries and transport, the direction of labour and the centralised control of education. In time, state communism (i.e. socialism) would yield to a stateless communism of economic abundance—'from each according to his ability, to each according to his needs'. The state, Engels wrote with the naive optimism of the true millenarian, would 'wither away'.

Let us return later to the communist view of the state. For now, I note only that socialism was supposed to lead towards 'communism', defined as a condition of universal abundance. None of the early Marxist prophets, Lenin included, named even an approximate date for the achievement of abundance. The closest any Soviet Communist came to it was in 1961, when Nikita Khrushchev presented the Programme of the 22nd Soviet Party Congress, which claimed that 'the threshold of communism' would be substantially reached by 1980. But 1980 has come and gone, and no more has been heard of the 1961 prediction, which was preposterous even by communist standards of prophetic accuracy.

In addition to this Utopian and unprovable vision of the future, the 22nd Congress Programme made a number of specific claims, which are worth recalling. One was that by 1970 Soviet Industrial production would surpass the American figure for 1961. This was perhaps a relatively modest claim, by millenarian standards, but the Programme went further by claiming that by 1970, the Soviet Union's industrial output *per head of the population* would surpass the American figure for the same year (1970). Again, the stated year came and went and no official spokesman in the USSR was noticeably in a hurry to recall the predictions of nineteen years earlier.

Two years before the 22nd Party Congress, the ebullient Mr Khrushchev had started the perilous habit of precise economic predictions, when he boasted in 1959 that by 1961, the Russians were going to produce more meat, butter and milk than the Americans. When the two years had elapsed, no more was heard of Khrushchev's boast. Indeed by the end of Khrushchev's decade of power (1954-64), the American farmer still produced seven or eight times as much as his Soviet counterpart. In milk and livestock, Soviet yields were only half the American.

It would not be worth recalling these dead claims of the recent past were it not for the fact that at the time many commentators (by no means all of them communists or even socialists) took them seriously. I shall be bringing this dismal picture up to date, but for now let us return to Lenin. The main difference between, say, the programme of Britain's Labour Party today and the programme of the triumphant Bolsheviks between 1917 and 1921 is that the Bolsheviks actually carried theirs through, because the Tsarist state had collapsed; they had absolute power and were ruthless enough to use it.

The day after Lenin had seized power, that is, on 7 November 1917, a Land Decree was published ordering the immediate partition of large estates, the land to be distributed among the peasants—who were not told that they would soon be herded into collective farms. On 19 February 1918, the nationalisation of the land was proclaimed. When the civil war threatened the towns with starvation, the peasants were ordered to turn over their entire surplus to the government. When the peasants demurred, the government ordered forcible requisitioning.

As soon as they were in power the Bolsheviks nationalised all the banks, confiscating private accounts and repudiating the national debt. As early as 28 November 1917, the workers were given control of their factories. In theory, the day of the soviets or workers' councils had dawned. But again, as with the peasants, the workers were not told that it would not be long before the party would take over from the soviets.

The reality was that the workers were ordered to join government-controlled trades unions and denied the right to strike (the argument— still in force, by the way, sixty-five years later—being that the workers would be striking against themselves, since they now owned their places of employment and the means of production). Compulsory labour followed, private trade was suppressed and the government rationed the distribution of food and commodities.

The outcome of this first, and admittedly brutal, dose of socialism was that by early 1921, the world's first 'workers' state' was in total economic collapse. How did Lenin cure the economic ills created by his own brand of socialism? Certainly not by more rigorous socialist methods. Instead, in March 1921, he launched the famous, but short-lived, New Economic Policy (NEP) which, while it lasted, was a partial return to private enterprise.

The government stopped helping itself to the peasants' food surplus. Instead, a grain tax was introduced, which enabled them to keep some of the surplus for themselves. Freedom of trade within the country was re-introduced and a new land statute was passed (in 1922) to permit small individual farms and even the use of hired labour. Some small industrial plants were returned to their former owners and private persons were allowed to start new enterprises. Private commercial establishments were also sanctioned in the cities and the financial system was reorganised on a semi-capitalist basis.

All this did not amount to the abandonment of socialism, since large industry stayed nationalised and foreign trade remained a state monopoly. Even this relatively modest return to a market economy, however, produced dramatic results. The great famine of 1921 had been caused, primarily, by drought, but it was aggravated by the economic collapse caused by socialism. Under the NEP, the national economy quickly sprang to life. In both industry and agriculture, output reached the pre-war levels and living standards, which had fallen drastically, recovered fast in town and country.

It is impossible to say whether Lenin would have drawn the obvious lesson from these circumstances (although one must assume that since he was a doctrinaire fanatic, he would have brushed them aside as an obstacle to his Utopian vision of the communist future). We shall never know for certain, as he died in January 1924.

The next two years went in the power struggle between Stalin and Trotsky, which Stalin won in 1926, when Trotsky was expelled from the party leadership.

As soon as Stalin had power in his own hands, he set about resuming the discarded socialist programme and forcing the pace of socialisation. The period of the famous (or notorious) Five-Year Plans began, on 1 October 1928. It is customary to date the Soviet Union's economic growth from that time, but some aspects of the situation are at times overlooked: such is the force of continuous propaganda.

The claim that it was Stalin's successive five-year plans which transformed the USSR from a backward peasant community to a great industrial power is partially true but in some respects a myth. For one thing, Russia was industrialising fast under the Tsars and was a net exporter of grain. Of course, the country was devastated by war, revolution and civil war. But it took the Bolsheviks ten years in power (1917–27) to reach the level of production Tsarist Russia had attained in 1914.

The remarkable growth achieved under the five-year plans was almost entirely in the sphere of heavy industry: in other areas growth was small or nil. The systematic neglect of the consumer started at that time, but the real disaster area was agriculture. Stalin wrecked Russian agriculture, strictly in pursuance of communist dogma requiring the collectivisation of the land. In 1932, the harvest was lower than in 1927. By 1933 half the country's livestock had been slaughtered or had died for lack of feed. Twenty years later, when Stalin died in 1953, Soviet agriculture stood roughly where the Tsar had left it during the Great War. Soviet citizens were eating less, and their diet was less nutritious than it had been twenty-five years earlier. Yet the price for this colossal non-achievement was appalling: five million peasants had been liquidated and millions more deported to the slave camps.

The obsession with heavy industry, which in effect has left the socialist fatherland far back in the race to abundance, needs a word of explanation.

There were three reasons for this initial decision, rigorously maintained through the long decades of communist socialism. Two make

THE TSAR'S CORNUCOPIA

STALIN'S CORNUCOPIA

sense of a kind; the third is difficult for non-communists to grasp, still less to accept as rational. The 'normal' reasons are these. Especially in the early days, the revolutionaries were building socialism for future generations to enjoy, and it was argued that the *Homo Sovieticus* of the future would enjoy the benefits of the fundamental capacity to be established in the first few years. The second reason was simply that it is far easier for a state-controlled economy to plan for heavy industry than for consumer industries. In a market economy, the consumers largely determine supply through their own needs and demands. But under socialism the consumer economy has been abolished by decree and it is too bad for the consumer if the central planners decide that he or she needs pig iron and steel (which you can neither eat nor wear).

The recondite third reason (which on reflection might even be the first in importance) was determined by Marxist doctrine. Marx had prophesied that the revolution would start in the most advanced industrialised countries. In fact, it started in relatively backward peasant Russia. *Post facto*, therefore, it was decided that Russia had to be industrialised fast, to justify the Marxian prophecy. This curious aberration is explained more fully in Robert Conquest's introduction to the important book by the Yugoslav dissident Milovan Djilas, *The New Class* (Allen and Unwin, 1966).

Under Stalin's forced industrialisation programme, the USSR became a formidable military power, as Hitler's hordes discovered. But the ordinary Soviet citizen's living standard remained pretty well static. The point is illustrated in the official Soviet statistics published in 1967 in anticipation of the fiftieth anniversary of the October Revolution. On 15 September that year, the Communist Party organ, *Pravda*, proclaimed that between 1913 and 1967, total industrial production increased 71 times; whereas in the same period the output of light industry rose only 17 times and of food production 14 times.

As with all Soviet statistics, these figures are suspect, although there is no reason to doubt the proportions cited. In 1913, according to Western calculations, the average Russian could buy about 40 per cent of what the average American could buy. By 1967, the average American could buy five times as much with his money as his predecessor of 1913. If, however, the average Soviet citizen in 1967 had 14 to 17 times as much food and consumer goods at his disposal as in 1913, then one might conclude that in 1967 real wages had caught up with the American level. But this was manifestly untrue. The fallacy is presumably a statistical one. In 1913, the bulk of the consumer goods available to Russians groaning under the Tsarist yoke came from the cottage industries, which are ignored by Soviet statisticians, who only consider Tsarist industrial output.

After twenty-five years of forced industrialisation under Stalin, living standards were no higher when he died than when he launched his first Five-Year Plan in 1928. I am, of course referring to the living standards of the ordinary soviet citizen and his family. Those of the *nomenklatura*— the establishment—were incomparably higher, with town flats and country dachas and access to foreign luxuries through special shops closed to outsiders (that is, to the bulk of the population).

Even under Stalin's iron hand, however, the output of the consumer industries was becoming more sophisticated and ordinary people were beginning to develop a taste for 'consumer durables', for cars, for washing machines, for cameras and watches. During the decades of terror and austerity, such hopes had been suppressed and the shoddy goods on offer were accepted because there was no choice. When Stalin died, his designated successor, Malenkov, made speeches calling for a new deal for the consumer. Khrushchev, having got rid of Malenkov, partly on the pretext that such views were heretical, took over Malenkov's approach as his own.

The problem was that tastes and demand had become more sophisticated, but the factories were still turning out the old shoddy stuff. The result was the great inventory crisis of the late 1950s and early 1960s, when vast stocks of goods began to accumulate because few people wanted to buy them. Nothing could better illustrate the fundamental shortcomings of socialism than this phase of Soviet economic history, which is quite distinct from communist violations of human rights. Prices were fixed arbitrarily by the army of planners in Moscow, who neither knew nor cared about the needs of the consumer. It was the planners who told the factories what to produce and how much of it. The planners fixed the production 'norms'. They might, for instance, decide that a particular year's target was 5 per cent more shoes, regardless of demand. There were penalties for failing to meet the norm and rewards for exceeding it. If vast quantities of shoes remained unsold, that was too bad: the norm had been met, or exceeded, in the absence of a market mechanism to test the real demand for shoes.

It was in these circumstances that a private delivery system sprang up and grew rapidly. It was, unfortunately, illegal, and the smart operator who made his profit by meeting consumer goods faced the penalties for unwanted success in a planned economy. In May 1961, Khrushchev extended the death penalty to various economic 'crimes': death to the freelance supplier.

In the early 1960s, a bold man started writing dangerously heretical articles, arguing that profits should be the index of the efficiency of an enterprise. His name was Professor Yevsei Liberman. The word 'profits' sent shudders through the offices of Gosplan, the Soviet centralised planning agency. The professor, however, was clever enough to express his views in strictly ideological terms, with frequent quotations from Marx and Lenin and repeated definitions of 'socialist' profits, which were ploughed back into the people's enterprises, and thence into the pockets of the deserving workers and managers, as distinct from capitalist profits, which, of course, went straight into the pockets of capitalist exploiters.

Professor Liberman's reward came in September 1965, when Premier Kosygin made proposals incorporating some of the Professor's reformist ideas. In January 1966 a pilot scheme was launched, when 43 enterprises in seventeen industries were brought into the 'profits' scheme. Each of the 43 had autonomy over its own show. By the end of 1968 more than 25,000 enterprises had switched to the reformed system. The results of this partial adoption of capitalist principles were gratifying. In 1966–7, industrial output rose by 20 per cent, and productivity by nearly 13 per cent.

Bold though the Liberman reform was, in its day, it could only be a palliative. It would have succeeded, in the full sense, only if socialist planning had been abandoned and the enterprises handed over to entrepreneurs. By definition, nothing of the kind could be envisaged, and the mountain of unsold goods began to accumulate again. Although big cuts in the prices of unsold goods were announced in April 1975, by October the total value of such stocks was estimated at 4.5 thousand million roubles, equal to about 2 per cent of the total retail trade. Simultaneously, private savings were rising dramatically. During the period of the Five-Year Plan launched in 1971, under Brezhnev, the *increase* in private savings amounted to nearly 70 per cent of accumulated savings. Why were Soviet citizens saving so much of their incomes? One reason, of course, was that the incomes had risen. But the main one was undoubtedly that they did not wish to buy the goods available in the shops.

It was in 1975, the last year of the 1971 Plan, that an alarming new trend began. In the first six months of 1975 the USSR quite suddenly, after a relatively good year, developed a phenomenal trade deficit of $1,400 million with the West. This reflected a fall of 3.5 per cent in Soviet exports to the West in the face of a rise of no less than 90 per cent in imports from the same countries.

This new situation was itself the outcome of the policy of 'détente' inaugurated by Leonid Brezhnev, whose advisers had persuaded him that the only way to draw level with and even overtake the United States in strategic military power, without too drastic a fall in Soviet living standards, was by making overtures to the West and attracting Western loans and credits on easy terms.

In the short term, at least, this policy was enormously successful. Western governments fell over each other in their eagerness to transfer high technology to the Soviets, and Western banks competed in the provision of money to enable the Soviets to pay for what they were getting. By the end of 1981, the net indebtedness of the USSR to Western banks had reached $19.5 billion (44 per cent higher than for 1980)—yet another indication of the long-term failure of Soviet socialism in comparison with the 'doomed' capitalist system.

Another sign of long-term socialist failure had come some years earlier, with the signature on 20 October 1975 of a five-year grain deal between the USSR and the USA, under which the Soviets committed themselves to buying at least six million metric tons of American grain between 1 October 1976 and 30 September 1981. The significance of this contract lay in its tacit recognition that they were no longer merely worried by the problem of an occasional poor harvest but by the continuing inability of the Soviet agricultural system to feed the population—after nearly sixty years of socialism.

In November 1982, the Soviet Union celebrated the 65th anniversary of the Bolshevik Revolution. There were slogans aplenty, including 'Glory to the CPSU' and 'We shall fulfil the 11th Five-Year Plan'. But the reality was that, according to Soviet statistics, labour productivity was *still* only 40 per cent of the American level (*SSR v tsifrakh v 1980 godu*, Moscow 1981, p.60). Moreover, the USSR was no longer even catching up. During the first nine months of 1982, labour productivity had risen by only 8.3 per cent over the same period in 1981. In certain key sectors (oil, iron and steel, non-ferrous metals, meat and the dairy industry), productivity had actually fallen (*Ekonomicheskaya Gazeta*, No. 44, October 1982).

It was the same old story. Soviet inventors had developed advanced automation systems. But the socialist planners had not found a way to mass-produce them. While the State Planning Committee and the Gas Ministry argued the toss, the oil and gas industry (to give an important example) was starved of advanced drilling equipment. That was Soviet socialism, 65 years after Lenin's coup.

It was also, of course, the inheritance of Yuri Andropov, the former head of the KGB, who took over as Party boss after the death of Brezhnev on 10 November 1982. I am not concerned here with Kremlinology, that abstruse semi-science which attempts, on inadequate evidence, to assess the changing balance of power within the top Soviet leadership. The point that interests us is the economic legacy, and the prevalence of corruption; and what, if anything, Andropov wanted or was able to do about these twin problems of Soviet socialist society.

The evidence of Andropov's first eight months in power suggests that the answer was going to be 'not much'. A lot of small fry were sacked or tried for minor corruption, such as the diversion of goods trains for the private sale of the goods being carried. But not much happened at the top.

The real problem was the economic system, in one word, socialism. In speeches and carefully leaked asides, Andropov let it be known that he was determined to modernise the economy, but even if his intentions were genuine, he was up against the accumulated inertia of decades. At 69, and apparently in poor health, it seemed doubtful whether he would muster enough energy to do more than tinker with the system.

In August 1983 a report prepared some four months earlier for the Kremlin leadership found its way into the Western press (*International Herald Tribune*, 4 August 1983). It called for a fundamental reform of the Soviet economy and asserted that its centralised management system could no longer ensure the 'full and effective use of the society's intellectual and labour resources'.

As *The Economist* pointed out that week (6 August), Andropov's experiment in 'reform', to date, was confined to two national ministries (out of more than 60), plus three smallish regions. The paper added: 'Now the staleness has started to creep back.' As my co-author, Arthur Seldon, has observed, socialism appears to be incurable. To be precise, it seems logically impossible to reform socialism and remain socialist. The only way out is to discard it outright. But the men in the Kremlin could hardly do that and hope to remain in power.

7

Socialism in Eastern Europe

Stalin imposed socialism on Eastern Europe by force of arms and political coercion. The Soviet dictator's economic ideas were, perhaps, rather primitive. He believed in autarky—self-sufficiency. Each satellite economy was to be a carbon copy of the Soviet original, with most of the investment going into heavy industry, while agriculture and the unfortunate consumer were neglected. In Khrushchev's day, a more sophisticated approach began. Autarky yielded to the 'international division of labour'. In other words, each country in the Soviet bloc was supposed to concentrate on whatever it could do best, to the benefit of the bloc as a whole, and of the Soviet Union in particular. The Soviet and satellite economic plans were co-ordinated through a body known as Comecon, but whose real name is the Council for Mutual Economic Aid.

As in Chapter 6, I am not concerned here with communist repression, although it can never be entirely ignored. Undoubtedly, political repression contributed to political dissatisfaction in Russia's East European dependencies. Without it, the shortages caused by socialist planning might have been borne more patiently by the people. And there was another important factor: the natural resentment of formerly independent nations against the colonial power.

At all events, the only uses of military power in Europe since World War II have been in Eastern Europe: the Soviet armed forces intervened in East Berlin in 1953 to suppress a workers' uprising; in Hungary in 1956; and in Czechoslovakia in 1968. Our concern here, however, is with the economic failure of socialism in all the countries of Eastern Europe without exception, the differences between them being of degree rather than kind.

Leaving aside the curious case of little Albania, which has followed its own course, and for some years was under Chinese, not Soviet influence, there are also two other exceptional cases to consider. One is Yugoslavia—the only country of Eastern Europe in which communism was imposed not by the advancing Soviet armies but by the victory of communist guerrilla forces commanded by a Croatian leader whose real name was Josip Boz, but who was better known as Marshal Tito. The other exception to the rule of universal Soviet domination has been Romania, which under its dictator Nicolae Ceausescu has managed to assert some independence in international affairs, while sticking to a strictly Stalinist repressive regime at home. The point that interests us here, however, is that in Yugoslavia, as in Romania, the economic system has to be described as 'socialist'.

There are people who doubt whether the Yugoslav economic system may correctly be so described. I am not among the doubters. Indeed, Yugoslavia's official name is the 'Socialist Federated Republic of Yugoslavia'. And the single ruling party describes itself, after several name changes, as the 'League of Communists of Yugoslavia'. The differences between the Yugoslav system and all other regimes of Eastern Europe are nevertheless substantial.

Socialist planning is less rigid in Yugoslavia than elsewhere. The basic principle is sometimes decribed as 'planned guidance'. There is a plan but the state does not directly administer the various economic enterprises. There is a fair amount of local autonomy, with a worker-management system in the factories, and co-operatives instead of rigid 'collectives' in agriculture. There is a free market for agricultural products and limited private enterprise on a self-management basis.

From a strictly Marxist standpoint, the Yugoslav economy is thus full of contradictions. One of the most paradoxical aspects of it, from a Soviet standpoint, is the fact that under Tito and his successors Yugoslavia in effect exports its unemployment problem by encouraging hundreds of thousands of Yugoslav workers to seek employment in the richer European countries, notably West Germany and Switzerland. One must not allow such paradoxes to carry one too far in assessing the character of the Yugoslav experiment. Foreign visitors are often told that the workers in Yugoslavia 'own' the factories they work in. It is not difficult to disprove this assertion. All that is needed is to put the question: 'If the workers own the factories, can they sell them and pocket the proceeds?' In fact, they cannot.

When Tito had his celebrated quarrel with Stalin in 1947–8, the Soviet dictator withdrew his hordes of advisers from Yugoslavia and Tito discarded the rigidities of Stalinist economics. As a result, the prosperity in any given factory or enterprise is determined by that horrid capitalist word, *profit*. There is a fair amount of private enterprise, and foreign capital investment has been allowed since Tito decided to join the General Agreement on Tariffs and Trade (GATT) in 1966.

These innovations have diluted socialism, but without turning Yugoslavia into a capitalist country. Certainly, the serious economic and financial crisis which came to a head in Yugoslavia in the summer of 1982 was remarkably similar to the simultaneous crises in other East European countries. In other words, it was a *socialist* crisis, not a capitalist one.

Tito died in May 1980, amid fears that the Soviet Union would attempt to reimpose its control over Yugoslavia now that its prestigious leader was out of the way. At the time of writing, Yugoslavia retains its independence. The economic crisis, however, had been building up while Tito was still alive. The extent of it became apparent when the League of Communists held its 12th Congress at the end of June 1982. There were heated debates on economic problems. The Prime Minister, Dusan Dragosavac, revealed in his main report that, at the end of 1981, Yugoslavia's hard currency debt stood at $20.1 billion. In 1982 alone, Yugoslavia had to find $5.3 billion-worth of hard currency simply to pay the interest. The repayments were going to eat up 27 per cent of hard currency earnings of some $18.5 billion from exports, tourism, shipping and the remittances of Yugoslavia's expatriate workers. Some weeks before the Congress, a special law had been passed enabling the government to seize most of the foreign currency earnings which until then had been under the control of individual Yugoslav companies. According to K.F. Cviic (in *The World Today*, London, of September 1982), of each $100 earned by an enterprise it could retain only $23.2.

Another speaker at the Congress, the new Foreign Trade Minister, Milenko Bojanic, revealed that $1.7 billion less would be available for imports of raw materials and machinery than in the previous year. In the January-May period of 1981, industrial production had increased by 3.5 per cent; in 1982 during the same period, the increase was only 1.6 per cent. For the first time since the final break with the Soviet Union in 1948, when Yugoslavia's former allies had imposed a total economic blockade, industrial output had actually dropped by 0.6 per cent. At the time of the Congress, many Yugoslav factories were sending their workers on compulsory leave. Some factories were going to close down permanently because of the shortage of hard currency for necessary imports. And all this against a background of 800,000 unemployed in a total labour force of just under 6 million in the 'socialist' sector of the economy (13.3 per cent).

The Romanian exception

Romania shares with Yugoslavia the distinction of being (though to a lesser degree) an exception to the rule of total subservience to Moscow. But in in economic terms the two countries are poles apart. Yugoslavia has diluted its socialism; Romania has stuck rigidly to the unimaginative original Stalinist model. The contrast between the two countries, indeed, provides a perfect illustration to my 'second Universal Rule of socialism': the more there is of it, the worse the failure.

The relative independence of Romania in international affairs is usually associated with the personality of Ceausescu, but his predecessor, Gheorghiu-Dej, started the process. Khrushchev, moving away from Stalin's autarky in favour of the 'international division of labour', had cast Romania in an agricultural role. Gheorghiu-Dej did not like this at all. As a small-scale carbon copy of the USSR, Romania had had a taste of industrialisation, and wanted more of it. Khrushchev called a meeting of Comecon to discuss his ideas for supra-national planning. Unexpectedly, the Romanian delegates declared that they would not accept supra-national planning. They were not against some co-ordination of national plans, but individual national interests had to be respected.

In mid-1963, the Soviets summoned the economic leaders of all member-states of Comecon to Moscow to discuss Romania's hostility to supra-national planning. The Romanians dug their heels in, and got their own way. By the time the next full meeting was held, in Prague at the end of January 1965, the East European power grid had been extended to Romania, a common pool of railway wagons had been set up and a joint oil pipeline completed.

Thereupon, Gheorghiu-Dej died, and Ceausescu stepped into his shoes on 22 March 1965. He continued to resist any attempts by Comecon to impose its rule upon his country. Instead, he improved Romania's economic links with Western countries, encouraging Western tourists to visit Romania and contribute to its economic development with their expenditure of hard foreign currencies.

As time went on, Ceausescu encouraged a 'cult of personality' to grow around him, the only rival of which in the communist world is the similar cult of the personality of the North Korean leader, Kim II Sung. The political implications of this cult need not concern us here, but it had unfortunate economic consequences. Western observers coined the term 'gigantomania' to describe some of Ceausescu's vast and unnecessarily ambitious projects, such as the construction of oil refineries with capacity three times as high as production would justify, and steel production facilities far in excess of Romania's capacity. Per capita, Romania by 1982 had become the second largest producer of steel in the world, next to the United States. Nobody knew quite what to do with the new Navodari oil refinery, the original purpose of which was to process Iranian crude for the European market. Nobody had the courage to call for a halt in the construction of a deep canal from the Danube to the Black Sea—a high-cost scheme which looked like turning out to be useless if European oil imports continued to be reduced by the search for alternative sources of energy. For all the expensive promotion, tourism proved an expensive flop. By mid-1982, a catastrophic shortage of basic foodstuffs had developed. Bread, flour, potatoes, green vegetables, cooking fats and meats had all but vanished. Even cornflour, at one time to be found in even the poorest households, had disappeared. Even for a Balkan country, corruption and the black market had reached unprecedented levels, and all efforts to control it through rationing and Draconian controls had failed. The plan was disastrously underfulfilled, and the harvest shortfall was nearly one-third.

Statistics made the economic picture look rosier than it really was. For instance, between 1950 and 1981, per capita income rose from $100 to $1,500, but the standard of living had not increased proportionately. In the 17 years to 1982, industrial production had risen on average 11.4 per cent a year, and five million new jobs had been created in industry since 1950. But the hard reality was that the government had cut the military budget by 10 per cent and was reduced to rationing private driving to alternate days, despite interminable queues at service stations.

As usual with a member of what Brezhnev called the 'Socialist Commonwealth', Romania in the depth of its economic crisis turned to the West for help. By the end of 1981, Romania's foreign debt had reached $9.6 billion—5.5 per cent up on the previous year. Final figures for 1982 were not available when this book was written, but were believed to have reached between $10 and $14 billion. As with other East European countries, Ceausescu asked the International Monetary Fund for a rescue loan—in his case for $300 million. As usual, with applicants for IMF loans, President Ceausescu was told to cut the growth of domestic spending, reduce imports and initiate various reforms. To this, his response was to sack his Prime Minister, Ilie Verdet, eight deputy premiers and several members of the Political Executive Committee. Whether Romania's economy was capable of reforming itself under Ceausescu's rigidly ideological rule remained an open question.

The rest

It is perhaps even more difficult to distinguish between communism and socialism in Eastern Europe than in the USSR itself. For Eastern Europe is, in the strictest sense, the colonial area. Stalin imposed Soviet-style communism on the 'liberated' countries of Eastern Europe by force and guile. With communist one-party rule came integral socialist economies. The local peoples had not asked for either. They got both.

East Germany is perhaps the most interesting case of all, because of the division of Germany, so that for fifteen years or so it was possible to compare 'capitalism' in West Germany with socialism in East Germany.

Germany as a whole had been devastated, so that both systems started out pretty well from zero. To be fair, East Germany's handicap was to be even worse than West Germany's, in that the Soviets under Stalin looted the areas they occupied on a grand scale—in the guise of 'war reparations'. (I am not here concerned with the morality of what they did, in the light of the devastation inflicted on the USSR by Nazi aggression. I am simply recording what happened.)

In the West, there was much doomsday talk, but relatively little action. In the East, Stalin just got on with it, unburdened by scruples. President Roosevelt's Secretary of the Treasury and personal friend, Henry J. Morgenthau, had called for the destruction of German industry and for the reduction of Germany to a pastoral economy. The 'Morgenthau Plan', as it was called, came to nought, however. Roosevelt died and Morgenthau resigned shortly after his death.

In the East, Soviet looting really was on a grand scale. During the brief period when the Red Army was in sole occupation of Berlin, the Soviets removed 75 per cent of all capital equipment. In those few months, machinery from some 1,900 industrial enterprises in the Soviet occupation zone was dismantled and shipped to Russia. It has been estimated that reparations to the Soviet Union in the post-war period amounted to 66.4 billion marks. Under Stalin's orders, all the industrial properties of 'war criminals', National Socialists (Nazis), and militarists were expropriated. In effect, private enterprise was simply eliminated from all large and most medium-sized industrial firms.

Stalin had hoped to extend 'socialism' to the whole of Germany, and nevertheless went easy over socialising measures in the Soviet occupation zone, seeking to reassure his wartime allies and persuade them to accept the reunification of Germany on his terms. It was not until the 'German Democratic Republic' emerged in 1949 that the imposition of socialism really got under way.

One of the first things the East German regime did was to confiscate all privately owned farms of more than 100 hectares. Ten years later—in 1959—about 52 per cent of the country's arable land had come under collective control. A new drive started in 1960 and by the end of the year, the regime could claim that agriculture was 98.7 per cent socialised. At the height of this drive, in one three-month period, about 340,000 farmers had been forced to join the co-operatives or had fled to the West.

The usual consequences followed. In 1969, the grain harvest dropped 12 per cent below that of the preceding year; there was a 30 per cent shortfall in potato and sugar beet crops. For years after 1964, East Germany was forced to buy more than one million tons of grain each year from the Soviet Union—until the Soviet Union itself ran into acute difficulties for exactly the same reason. Both East Germany and the Soviet Union thereupon started buying grain on a large scale from the 'capitalist' United States.

Forced industrialisation on the Stalinist pattern created further economic difficulties for East Germany. As usual, centralised planning created anomalies. One whopping error was the construction of a huge steel combine at Stalinstadt, which cost $600 million, yet proved unable to produce anything except crude pig iron. As with other East European countries, East Germany's development under socialism was hampered by the requirements of Comecon as a whole. For example, plans to develop Rostock as a major sea port and shipbuilding centre were suspended, because Comecon had decided that competition from Rostock could harm the Polish port of Szczecin (formerly Stettin). The aircraft industry was simply dropped. Textile plants and motor car factories were held back. On the other hand, a giant uranium mining complex, employing 140,000 workers, was maintained at the Wismuth Aktiengesellschaft purely to provide for Soviet needs.

In striking contrast, once the Western Allies had given the job of Director of Economic Council for the Joint Anglo-American district to Dr Ludwig Erhard in 1948, the West Germany economy took off rapidly. Erhard believed in free enterprise and the market economy. He began by sweeping away most price and wage controls and by abolishing rationing. The socialist economists were scandalised, but he stood his ground. Almost overnight, the factories were in production, the black markets vanished and the shops were filled with goods. Within a year, the national income in real terms was back to the 1936 level. There was a temporary increase in unemployment, which reached 11 per cent in 1950; but it then declined steadily to only 0.8 per cent in 1961. Erhard swept away rent controls and reduced income tax. Between 1949 and 1977, West Germany maintained the lowest inflation rate among industrial countries—only 2.7 per cent. This was the 'German miracle'.

In their millions, East German men, women and children fled to the West, 'voting with their feet', as Lenin once said in a different context. Altogether West Germany had to absorb some 14 million refugees. Admittedly, many of these came from what had been East Germany— the lands absorbed by Poland in compensation for territory seized by Stalin under the Nazi–Soviet pact of 1939. However, East Germany was being bled white by the decision of nearly 30,000 citizens, *every month*, to leave their Socialist paradise and seek to better themselves under the booming economy of West Germany. To be sure, these dissatisfied East German citizens were also fleeing the rigours of Communist repression. The point is that they preferred to drop everything, leave their homes, and take themselves and their families to 'capitalist' West Germany. To stem the flow, Khrushchev (who had succeeded Stalin) built the Berlin Wall—a hideous line of concrete and barbed wire with lethal devices, to keep the citizens of East Germany within its borders. Despite this stemming of the drain of East German brain and skills, the growth rate of the East German economy declined after the building of the wall.

If the regime's statistics are to be believed, growth had reached the exceptional figure of 12.4 per cent in 1959, and the East German leaders were emboldened to prophesy that by 1961 they would surpass West Germany in per capita production. But the growth rate declined to 8 per cent in 1960, then to 6.2 per cent during 1961, settling down thereafter to an average of about 6 per cent. Needless to say, the East German regime did not overtake the performance of the German Federal Republic. A further boast that it would do so by 1975 also failed to materialise. It is interesting to note, nevertheless, that the well-known qualities of the German people—in hard work and organisation—did assert themselves in East as well as West Germany, so that the East Germans—in spite of socialism—achieved the highest living standards in the Soviet bloc, and became the tenth industrial power in the world.

In each of the East European upheavals (including Poland in the 1980s), economic as well as political factors played a part. In East Berlin and in Hungary, for instance, the workers had been growing more and more fed up because of the system of workers' norms—that is, quotas of work—which had been imposed in the factories. Every so often norms were raised, which automatically reduced the wages of the majority of the workers. As I said earlier, it is not easy to distinguish between communism and socialism in these matters. Obviously, the decision to raise norms was a political one. But one of the purposes was to screw more output out of the workers—an economic purpose. From the workers' point of view, the effect was economic. They felt they were being made poorer and poorer. Ironically, it was under communism that the workers were being 'pauperised'—whereas Karl Marx had forecast the pauperisation of the workers under capitalism. Then the workers, having had enough of this new form of exploitation, started rioting in the streets; and that was a *political* action on their part.

More purely economic factors played their part in the upheavals in Czechoslovakia and Poland, although it would be wrong to exaggerate their importance in comparison with resentment at the injustices of arbitrary rule.

There is a monotonous sameness about the economic ills of the 'Socialist Commonwealth'—understandably, since they stem from the same causes. In happier times, the economy of Czechoslovakia had been relatively advanced and well balanced. Then came centralised planning and the usual zeal for large-scale production of capital goods. The result, by the mid-1960s, was a superficially impressive economic boom which went on for about a decade. It was a defective boom, for while heavy industry was growing, light industry, consumer goods and agriculture were declining fast.

By 1963, there was a serious recession. Czech technology—at one time well able to hold its own with that of the West—started dropping well behind. The 'Prague Spring' of 1968 was a revolt of the intellectuals, and of a part of the Communist Party itself, against local oppression and subservience to Moscow. But a stagnant and unbalanced economy made its contribution to the gathering ferment.

There is an interesting contrast between the economic policies of Hungary and of Czechoslovakia after their respective upheavals. The Hungarian approach was certainly the more enlightened. After the brutal and bloody repression of 1956, the government of Janos Kadar gradually relaxed the rigous of Communist rule, both politically and economically. In agriculture—there as elsewhere in the bloc, a disaster area—incentives for the farmers were increased, so that by the late 1970s, the country was again self-sufficient in food, as it had been before the war. In industry, the regime decided to borrow heavily from the Yugoslavs, with a good deal of local autonomy for individual factories, and the introduction of a market system for prices.

By mid-1970, the central planners had surrendered their control to a large extent. At the time of the failed revolution in 1956, they controlled something like one million prices. Fourteen or 15 years later, only 1,000 prices were centrally determined. As a result, by all accounts, the atmosphere in Hungary was relatively relaxed and the Hungarians were more inclined to smile and laugh than their neighbours.

In Czechoslovakia, Gustav Husak, the austere party man who took over when the Soviets had deposed his hapless predecessor, Alexander Dubcek, did make some material concessions, but seemed afraid of going too far along the Yugoslav path. In politics, incidentally, he made no concessions at all and the regime remained highly repressive. Some observers of the Czechoslovak scene described what happened as a kind of 'unwritten social contract': dreams of political reform were shelved, in return for greater material comforts. Personal consumption rose by 27 per cent during the 1971–5 plan period. Real wages rose by more than 5 per cent. The private automobile—that symbol of affluence—came into its own. In 1971, only one person in 17 owned a car. By 1975, it was one in 10, and in 1979 one in eight.

In Poland, economic difficulties came in waves. On a number of occasions, workers' riots caused political changes. The workers' riots in Poznan in June 1956 brought a change of party leadership four months later, when Wladyslaw Gomulka came to power. But Gomulka himself was forced to step down after similar riots in December 1970. His successor, Edward Gierek, promptly announced a 'new development strategy'. Capital and technology would be imported from the West, to be paid for by increased production in Poland itself. Instead, Poland found itself relying more and more on ever-growing Western credits, without any visible means of repaying debts thus contracted. In 1976 came more workers' riots. Four years or so later, generalised unrest led to the emergence of the independent trade union group calling itself Solidarity, which for a time competed with the officially sponsored trades unions.

In agriculture, incidentally, Poland was the exception to the communist rule. After the failed revolution of 1956, all serious attempts to collectivise agriculture were abandoned, so that about 70 per cent of Polish farms to this day remain in private hands. In principle, this reliance on the private sector ought to have made a vast contribution to the agricultural sector. However, the ruling party retain full control of incentives, grain feed for cattle and fertilisers. Individual farmers owned the land they tilled, but have no control over their own destinies. The advantages of private farming were thus largely denied to the country.

When the great oil crisis of 1973–4 hit the West, with massive price increases decreed arbitrarily by the oil-producing countries' cartel known as OPEC, the regimes of Eastern Europe felt smugly protected. The USSR was their main supplier, and the regimes of Comecon felt secure. A rude awakening was on its way. The Soviet Union increased its sales of oil to the West, and simultaneously raised its prices for East European importers. By 1980, Czechoslovakia, for instance, was paying nearly five times as much per ton of Soviet oil as in 1970. The 'oil shock' of the late 1970s thus made its unwelcome contribution to the deepening economic crisis in Eastern Europe. Not one of the Comecon countries was able to meet its planned targets during the years 1976 to 1980. Most of them experienced severe food shortages. Poland and Romania had been net exporters of grain, but had to start importing it. Food rationing was introduced in both those countries. In 1981, East Germany's grain imports from the United States cost some $370 million. One outcome was drastic increases in food prices in the East European countries. In Czechoslovakia, for instance, the price of meat had hardly changed for two decades. Then, on 30 January 1982, the party decreed a rise of 41 per cent. About the same time, Romania raised the prices of more than 200 food items by 35 per cent on average. In Poland, the rise was quite staggering: an average increase of 241 per cent in food prices as a whole, decreed and announced on 1 February 1982.

A mountain of debt

Perhaps the most striking illustration of the inferiority of socialist economics, as compared with the economics of free enterprise and the market, was the growing mountain of debt accumulated by the Eastern bloc during the late 1970s. The fact that certain important non-communist countries (such as Brazil, Mexico and Venezuela) were also seriously indebted to Western banks made no difference. It was the socialist system as a whole that was in crisis and had turned to the West for help—not the other way round. The communist theorists were fond of talking about the supposed 'general crisis of capitalism'. The reality was a general crisis of communism and its socialist economic systems.

In June 1982 Comecon issued official figures for the level of debt of its component members at the end of 1981. The overall figure was $80.7 billion. The net indebtedness to Western banks of the USSR itself was shown as $19.5 billion (44 per cent higher than for 1980). Per capita, Poland was well ahead: $24 billion (136 per cent up). The Hungarians and Romanians had performed better, but only in comparison. Hungary was regarded by Western academics as having the best-managed economy in Eastern Europe, but that was not saying very much. The Comecon figures showed an accumulated Hungarian debt of $7.8 billion for 1981 (5.4 per cent up on 1980). Romania's foreign debt stood at $9.6 billion (5.5 per cent up on the previous year) and was rising rapidly.

It was fair to note that during the same period, the economies of the major Western powers were in deep recession—the most severe of its kind since the Great Depression of the 1930s. The point, however, was that Socialism was supposed to produce abundance, and to avoid the recurrent crises of Western economic systems. Clearly, on the evidence of the Eastern bloc's own economists and statisticians, it did neither.

8

Far Eastern Models—and Cuba

By my own self-denying discipline, there is very little to be said in this book about socialism in China, North Korea and Vietnam. But rather more about Cuba.

The reason why I have relatively little to say about the three Far Eastern countries is simple: in all three, the *communist* element, as distinct from that of *socialist* planning, is overwhelming. In all three, again, the irrational element of mad dictatorship is strong. All three are totalist tyrannies of the worst kind. Worse than the USSR by my rule-of-thumb about such regimes: can the ordinary man or woman (i.e. *not* members of the ruling party) opt out of politics? In the Soviet Union, opting out is possible, up to a point. In China under Mao, opting out was virtually impossible: the ubiquitous street committees saw to that. If anything, North Korea is worse. As for Vietnam, the message of recent visitors is that to some extent the inhabitants of Ho Chi Minh City (which used to be Saigon) can get away with a bit of freelancing on the side, by native wit and because the communists did not overrun this southern capital until 1975. North Vietnam, in contrast, has had full-scale communist control since 1954, and a good dose of subterranean communism since 1945, spreading gradually during the unhappy First Indochina War, involving the French.

In this bunch, Cuba might seem the odd man out, and in a way it is. All four of the examples in this chapter, however, do have something in common: all three are, or were, peripheral countries in the great communist empire. China broke away. North Korea, under its own mad dictator, is not exactly a Soviet satellite. Vietnam is. And so is Cuba.

The Great Helmsman

The leaders of communist countries tend to concentrate great powers in their hands, and to become the centre of a 'cult of personality'. They become gods. Their likeness, on a gigantic scale, is displayed everywhere, in picture form or in sculpture.

Of no communist country was this truer than of the Chinese People's Republic. Such was the build-up of the personality of the leader of the Chinese Revolution, Mao Tse-tung, that the image of 'the Great Helmsman' (as he liked to be called) was accepted in countries that ought to have known better. (The sycophantic obits in the Western press when the Great Helmsman died in 1976 made, for me at least, nauseating reading.)

Whether he or Stalin was the greater mass murderer is difficult to determine. This is not, however, the aspect of Maoism that concerns us here. The reason why China under Mao does not have much to teach us about *socialism* in action is that on two separate occasions the Great Helmsman, in fulfilment of his private follies, utterly wrecked the Chinese economy.

The first occasion was in 1958, when Mao launched what he called the 'Great Leap Forward'; from which the long-suffering Chinese fell flat on their faces. Until then, by the tenets of socialist planning in a relatively primitive economy, the Chinese Communists had not done too badly. They were producing quite a lot of steel—about three times as much as India when disaster struck—and by mobilising mass peasant labour they were doing pretty well with flood control and other desirable tasks. Moreover, although the agricultural performance was not exactly brilliant, at least distribution had improved. The people were not exactly the best-fed in the world, but there was some substance to the official claim that famine had been abolished. Mass campaigns had virtually wiped out flies and sparrows, and disease was on the retreat.

Then Mao went haywire. Not for him the distant mirage of communism— abundance for all—the image of plenty that retreated just as you thought you were drawing near to it. Besides, he was tired of listening to the Russians, whose technicians, in those days, swarmed over the vast country. He was going to bring in communism *now*, in his own lifetime.

In 1957, when this bold idea occurred to the great leader China's population was already estimated at 600 million. This was 'the people' and there was nothing, but nothing, which 'the people' could not do, in its collective genius. A tremendous, unified effort, mobilising all 600 million hard-working Chinese would at a bound carry the People's

Republic forward over the threshold of 'communism', leaving Russia far behind.

Almost overnight, the 750,000 collective farms were merged into vast communes—26,000 of them—in which the individual would sink virtually without trace.

The peasants ate in huge communal messes, and the sexes were segregated in vast dormitories, with one room reserved for husbands and wives to get together at predetermined times for procreative duties.

But the greatest effort of all was to go in building, virtually overnight, a gigantic steel industry. All over the country, workers and peasants were exhorted to build 'backyard furnaces'. As the year wore on (1958), the Party kept on raising production targets. Mao's approach was pure hysteria and mysticism. He had decided that China no longer needed scientists or technicians. The collective genius of 'the people' was all that was needed and the hapless scientists and technicians, together with 'intellectuals', were put to work in the fields. Fertiliser was short, but what did that matter?—each Chinese was his own fertiliser factory.

The final outcome, as might have been predicted, was economic disaster on an incredible scale. The rail system, already inadequate, had been totally disrupted through moving 'steel' from place to place. Food supplies became uncertain. To please the Great Helmsman, local Party bosses had faked all production figures. A steel output of 11 million tons had been claimed. Now, the shamefaced bosses admitted that not more than 8 million tons of the stuff was truly steel: the rest was unusable. A grain harvest of 375 million tons had been claimed. In 1959, it was admitted that the true figure did not exceed 250 million. And so on. In December 1958, Mao Tse-tung resigned as Chairman of the Republic (though he remained as Chairman of the Communist Party).

The next great disaster which Mao inflicted on the Chinese people started in 1966, and was termed the 'Great Proletarian Cultural Revolution'. It lasted about four years, and as a man-made disaster was even worse than the Great Leap Forward.

There is no space here to describe this period of madness, when young people were turned against their elders, encouraged to destroy as much of China's immemorial culture as they could, to humiliate or actually kill members of the vast bureaucracy that held the country together.

Mao's purpose was to get rid of his rivals, especially the 'perfect communist', Liu Shao-ch'i, who had replaced him as Chairman of the Republic, and the Central Committee's Chairman, Teng Hsiao-p'ing.

Teng in particular, was disgraced and Mao coined a choice insult for him: he was branded a 'capitalist roader'. But with Mao dead, Teng came back and gradually made himself the most powerful man in People's China.

He even proved, within limits, that Mao's insult fitted him, for in his attempt to bring some prosperity to the sorely tried Chinese people, he went so far as to encourage Chinese entrepreneurs from Hong Kong to build factories in South China and do busines. Undoubtedly China in 1983 is a far more relaxed, less tormented country than it was under Mao. Less totalist, too, in that it has even become possible to 'opt out' so long as one does not actively oppose the system.

To what extent China will flourish under the pragmatic socialism of Teng and his associates is hard to say. What can be said is that the condition of mainland China has all along provided a dismal contrast with the bustling success and prosperity of the Chinese who are fortunate enough to live under the Nationalist regime on the island of Taiwan, or for that matter in colonial Hong Kong. But that is another story, beyond the scope of this book.

North Korea

The same illuminating contrast may be observed between the regimented austerity of communist North Korea and the almost unbelievable prosperity achieved in a remarkably short time with capitalist methods in South Korea. The divided countries, indeed, constitute living proof of the superiority of the market economy and free enterprise over centralised socialist planning. What is true of People's China on the one hand, and Taiwan and Hong Kong on the other, is equally true of the two Koreas and of East and West Germany.

In North Korea, however, the element of communism and of dictatorial irrationality are, if anything, even stronger than in China under Mao, so that precise lessons about *socialism* as such are hard to draw. Under Kim Il Sung, North Korea has had, by general expert consensus, the most tightly regimented society on earth. Again, it has developed, more than any other communist country—the Soviet Union not excepted—a *permanent war economy*. Finally, it shares with Romania under Ceausescu the dubious honor of fostering the most extravagant cult of personality of them all.

These are communist rather than socialist characteristics. A country ruled for more than four decades by a megalomaniac planning a war of revenge is hardly a fair model of socialism. And I do want to be fair.

Vietnam

The case of Vietnam is not much more relevant to this little study. It has not (since the death of the founder of the Democratic Republic, Ho Chi Minh, in 1966) been afflicted by a cult of personality. But it is a country which, except for two years or so after the First Indochina War ended in 1954, has been continuously at war since 1946. And although the Americans withdrew in 1973 and the communists overran the south two years later, Vietnam is *still* at war. Twice since then, it has been invaded by neighbouring China. And for the past few years, it has itself invaded its smaller neighbour Kampuchea (formerly Cambodia), where fighting continues to this day.

When every allowance is made for these extraneous circumstances, however, enough residue is left to enable one to attribute some at least of Vietnam's economic troubles to socialism and to the kind of problems socialism brings in its train: bad planning, corruption, poor management. To these should now be added *unacceptability*. The northerners have had a prolonged dose of socialism, with the usual repression, and the slaughter of at least 50,000 and possibly 100,000 peasants during the 'land reform programme' in the 1950s. The relatively easy-going southerners had got used to relative prosperity, first under the French and later with the arrival of American forces in large numbers. The victorious northerners brought socialism with them, and the southerners do not like it, and have not had time to lump it or to forget happier times, even when earlier wars were raging.

The International Monetary Fund (IMF), reporting in 1982 on the economic situation in Vietnam, reported that *per capita* income had fallen from $241 a year in 1976 to $153 in 1981.

In March that year, the General Secretary of the ruling Party, Le Duan, reporting to its 5th Congress, admitted that some of the 'many acute problems' facing the economy stemmed from 'shortcomings and mistakes' by the party itself and by state officials. The population was growing faster than output, and there were shortages in food and essential consumer goods, including clothing. 'Large numbers of working people' were not being employed, and many enterprises were operating below capacity. As is so often the case with socialism, there was little discernible relationship between planning and achievement. The IMF figures showed that industry had grown by only 1.9 per cent in 1981—whereas the Plan had called for a 4–5 per cent rise. In agriculture, the Plan had decreed a 6–7 per cent rise, but actual growth was only 3.2 per cent.

In French colonial times, Vietnam was a major rice-exporting country in South-East Asia, along with Burma and Thailand. In 1981, however, despite a record harvest of 15 million tonnes of food grains (including 12.5 million tonnes of rice), the Vietnamese still needed to import 1.3 million tonnes. The classic situation of agriculture in communist/ socialist regimes was developing fast. In 1981, food production fell by 230,000 tonnes in South Vietnam—mainly because incentives were poor and southern peasants had started growing only what they themselves needed. The regime was planning to collectivise most of the south by 1985, yet by mid-1982, less than 12 per cent of arable land was worked by the collectives.

In financial terms, Vietnam stood in relation to the Soviet bloc much as the Soviet bloc stood in relation to the West. By March 1982, Vietnam's total foreign debts had reached about $3,500 million, about two-thirds to the USSR and Eastern Europe, and the rest to OECD countries.

As one of the 'poor relations' of the communist world, Vietnam was exporting much of its labour to the Soviet bloc. Probably up to half a million Vietnamese are now working in the USSR, Czechoslovakia, Bulgaria and the German Democratic Republic (East Germany). Many of them appear to have been drafted for work on the Siberian pipeline to Western Europe—exchanging the humid heat of South Vietnam for the permafrost of the Soviet tundra. Hundreds of thousands more have taken to sea in rickety boats, to seek economic or political refuge in the West, many of them dying before having reached their objectives.

Castro's Tropical Paradise

Along with socialism, Cuba offers quite a lot to its people: a flourishing cult of the outsize personality of its *Lider máximo*, Fidel Castro, and wars of foreign conquest as surrogate forces for the Soviet Union, mainly in Africa. It is also a major instigator and participant in political insurgencies in the Caribbean and elsewhere in Latin America.

Surrogate wars are as costly as other kinds, but on this score, Castro has little to worry him: the bills are picked up by his Soviet protectors. In the 1980s, the best Western estimates were that Cuba was costing the

USSR about $1 million a day—roughly the same as that other remote-control satellite in Vietnam. Again, however, our concern here is not with the communist aspects of the regime, but with the performance of centralised socialist planning. Let the Cuban leaders themselves do the talking.

Fidel Castro seized power by force of arms in January 1959, having driven the dictator Batista into exile. Slightly more than twenty years later, in an extraordinary speech before the Cuban National Assembly on 27 December 1979, he reported candidly on the state of the economy after two decades of socialism. Usually, Castro—who is prone to make speeches of inordinate length—seeks the maximum publicity for whatever he says. In this case, he imposed an unprecedented ban on any reporting of it in the Cuban media. The text nevertheless leaked out, as in 1956 Khrushchev's famous 'secret speech' in Moscow had leaked out. The main points were these:

> Admitting widespread problems, he blamed inefficiency and dishonesty, but also the weather and 'imperialists'. He admitted that Cuba's problems could no longer be blamed on the inexperience of the original revolutionaries.

'During 1979 there were difficulties and shortcomings in connection with imports from the socialist area... by October, only 28 per cent of the 500,000 cubic metres of wood due to be received by us in the year had reached us ... you can imagine how much this has affected everything, principally buildings, furniture production, the production of packing cases. Wood is not an edible product; it is not eaten. But it affects the economy.'

'This year 1979 was one of the worst from the point of view of the fulfilment of deliveries, even affecting the socialist area, in spite of their efforts to comply with delivery.'

'... there are already about 1,200,000 television sets in the country with 200,000 per year now being available. You might say; 'Would it not be better to import more towels and fewer television sets? More sheets and fewer television sets?' ... that is what we cannot do, because the choice is not available. The friendly countries which supply us with television sets do not have towels or sheets or mattresses to export. On the other hand, they have television sets, so we import television sets.'

'There are no towels because, of a production of 3,600,000, so many are allocated for social expenditure and only so many remain for the population, that one only gets a new towel once every so many years.'

'If they (the Russians) have forests which they cannot exploit because they do not have the work force, they should make them over to us, even if they are in Siberia; and in Siberia better, because it is not so hot there. And we could send our work brigades to produce wood in Siberia so that we would have all the wood we need at our disposal . . . as our forests do not have wood and Siberia's forests have, if the USSR is our sister—and she is—then those resources are also ours.'

'We, who have had tens of thousands of workers and international fighters abroad, with 1,200 teachers in Nicaragua, . . . we, who at a given time, have had 36,000 soldiers in Angola, who at another time have had up to 12,000 soldiers in Ethiopia, we who now have builders in Angola, in the Republic of Guinea, in Libya, in Iraq, and who have had them in Vietnam, how are we not going to have 10,000 men if we need them?'

'Our labour laws today really are protecting the delinquent: in essence our legal system is protecting the delinquent, the vagabond and the absentee; it is not protecting the good worker, who suffers in all this.'

'Anyone who sees an illegal electric line must report it even though it be his first cousin, even though it be his brother who has installed a new illegal electric line; report it and cut it. It is also the task of judges and public prosecutors, and I say to them: 'You are imposing fines that are too light, and that cannot be.'

Castro added that the whole system must be tightened up and revolutionary fervour revived against ideological enemies.

A year later, in December 1980, Fidel Castro made three major speeches. He was mainly concerned with the possibility of an invasion from the United States, President Reagan having just been elected. The invasion did not, of course, materialise, but all three of Castro's December speeches were permeated with excuses for failures, promises of improvement and exhortations to improve quality and quantity. He dwelt on the impending shortfall in the sugar crop, damage to the tobacco crop, African swine fever and the need for energy conservation. He gave a thinly veiled picture of poverty and under-nourishment with distribution difficulties of coffee, rice and cornmeal. The pace of industrialisation, he said, was too slow; labour discipline needed to be strengthened, as did job incentives. Transport was inadequate, with too few taxis and chaotic bus services. A date celebrated with special fervour each year in Cuba is 26 July. That day in 1953, Castro had made a first but abortive attempt to overthrow Batista. On 26 July 1982, he made his usual speech, this time to mark the 29th anniversary of the failed attempt. He made as much as he could of ambitious plans to raise the sugar crops from about 8 million tonnes in 1980 to 10 million tonnes by 1985, and to boost the production of nickel—another hard currency earner for Cuba—from 42,000 tonnes to 100,000 tonnes annually by late 1984. That was the *good* news—all in the future. The bad news concerned the present and recent past. He revealed that Cuba's debt to the West stood at about $3,500 million, while there was an overall trade deficit of $1,400 million, more than half of it with the USSR. He foresaw the abandonment of some projects, short-time working in some industries and virtually no economic growth. Not entirely unfairly, he blamed the country's problems on the low world price for sugar (80 per cent of Cuba's export earnings) and the cost of servicing debts to the West.

Two years earlier, in 1980, Castro's government had carried out a special survey of economic performance. It had found that 90 per cent of manufactured goods did not measure up to quality control standards. Some 41 per cent of managers in the sugar industry were untrained. Vehicle maintenance was poor and there was a chronic lack of spare parts. In ten years, living standards had hardly progressed at all.

That, too, was socialism (Third World-style).

9

Third World Socialism

Overwhelmingly, the leaders of the 'emerging' countries opted for socialism when they had won independence or had it conferred upon them by departing colonial powers. Invariably, the option has proved disastrous.

Yet the reasons for the choice are easy to understand: they were political and psychological, never economic.

During the 'struggle' for independence, the new leaders found a sympathetic hearing for their claims and aspirations among Western communists and socialists. The communists were, of course, interested parties, hoping to set the free colonies of the West on the communist path and bring them into the Soviet orbit. The socialists were more disinterested, in the true sense, but naturally inculcated their ideology into the gratefully receptive minds of their colonial protégés.

As for the said protégés, once they came to power or were in sight of it, the option of socialism became a hard-headed calculation. A centralised economy and a growing bureaucracy became natural devices to perpetuate their hold on power. The economics of 'capitalism' and of the marketplace would have deprived them of control over large and probably growing sectors of the population. Thus gratitude, intellectual laziness and cynical expediency combined to foster the installation of socialism.

There was another factor. Capitalism was identified with imperialism, in the minds of the new leaders, heavily influenced by Lenin's historically absurd analysis of imperialism as the final phase of capitalism (there were empires before capitalism existed; and the largest surviving empire, in the 1980s, is that of the communist-socialist Soviet Union). The adoption of socialism thus became a moral, or at any rate a political, necessity.

LIBERATION

There are so many examples. India's Jawaharlal Nehru was naturally in tune with the rather vague socialism of a Kingsley Martin, for so many years identified with the Hampstead leftism of his *New Statesman*. Indonesia's Ahmed Sukarno thought of himself as a socialist, although his interest in economics was minimal. At all events, the *idea* of socialism was compatible with his notions of financial profligacy and the cult of his own personality. The same was true of Kwame Nkrumah of Ghana.

Under its original post-independence leader, U Nu, Burma had turned towards socialism. Unfortunately, General Ne Win, the man who ousted him in 1958 then again in 1962 (having briefly returned power to the civilian politicians) travelled in the same sterile direction. Julius Nyerere of Tanzania tried his own version of socialism which he called *ujamaa* ('familyhood'). It was perhaps even more disastrous than others mentioned.

In French-speaking Africa, too, a number of the new leaders opted for socialism. One was Sékou Touré of Guinea. Another was Modibo Keita of Mali. Even the legendary Leopold Senghor of Senegal, poet and erudite grammarian (who polished the draft of France's Constitution for the Fourth Republic), declared his country to be on the socialist path. He defined socialism, with closer regard for political sentiment than for the truth, as 'the rational organisation of human society according to the most scientific, the most modern and the most efficient methods'. Fortunately, he was less doctrinaire in practice than verbally.

It has to be noted that, by African standards, 'capitalist' Kenya is incomparably more prosperous than socialist Tanzania, or Zambia. In French-speaking Africa, the prosperity of free enterprise Ivory Coast, under the wise and pragmatic leadership of Felix Houphouët-Boigny, stands in glaring contrast to its poverty-stricken socialist neighbours. Similarly, in Asia, the high living standards of the island republic of Singapore, which has no resources other than its skills and harbour facilities, stands out against the grey drabness of the socialist countries, including Burma. If Taiwan and the giant economy of Japan are introduced into the comparison, the failures of socialism, for instance in India, are dazzlingly clear.

Case-studies

India
Nehru and his associates were perhaps social democrats rather than

socialists (whereas his daughter, Mrs Indira Gandhi, and deferred successor as India's Prime Minister, is a socialist rather than a social democrat, and correspondingly more authoritarian). This meant that his attachment to parliamentary democracy was genuine; which in turn meant that his government's doses of socialism always stopped short of being lethal.

In my book on independence (*The Morning After*, 1963), I made a comparative study of Chinese and Indian socialist planning. In the grip of Mao Tse-tung's form of totalism, the Chinese People's Republic rushed headlong into the great social and economic disaster of 'the great leap forward' (described earlier). Nehru's attachment to democracy, and a character that fell well short of Mao's ruthlessness, protected India from the worst consequences of unbridled socialism.

In 1951, three years after independence, Nehru launched India's first five-year plan. The goals were fairly modest, and luck came in the shape of favourable monsoons and excellent harvests in 1953–4 and 1954–5. Irrigation made great strides, and the so-called Community Development Programme seemed to be working towards its goal of making India self-sufficient in food. Real national income rose by more than 18 per cent, and real per capita income by nearly 11 per cent. The rate of investment was 'normal' for hitherto static economies of the Indian kind: it rose during the first-year plan (1951–6) from 4.0 per cent of the national income to more than 7 per cent.

The second plan was far more ambitious, and far more socialist, than the first. The lion's share of new investment was earmarked for the public sector: £2,850 million, compared to £1,800 million for the private sector. Admittedly there was a case for heavy investment in the public sector, for apart from the railways—one of the great legacies of the British Raj—India was woefully short of infrastructure—of roads, power stations, schools, training schools.

Then as at all stages of India's history, before and after independence, the great, uncontainable problem was the soaring population. Between 1956 and 1961, the planners had calculated that some 10 million new workers would be looking for jobs. And they knew that it was far beyond the capacity of India's primitive agriculture to absorb them. Industrialisation seemed the answer; although it was of course typical of socialist planning that it was assumed that private enterprise and the law of supply and demand were too 'risky' to be trusted to fill the need.

In the event, private enterprise, though relatively starved of funds by the planners, did spectacularly better than public. In the ten years of the first two plans, the output of the private enterprises had soared by anything between 350 and 1,000 per cent. India had become an important manufacturing nation, producing a range of goods from bicycles to diesel-electric motors, from sewing machines to refrigerators both for the home market and for export. Overall, industrial output had risen between 110 and 120 per cent. Great strides had been made in communications and electrification, in irrigation and fertilisers, in oil and machine-tools.

The shortcomings, however, typified the irresponsible optimism of bureaucrats planning a country's economic development from the centre. There were, for instance, perilously optimistic assumptions about where the money was to come from to meet the bills, and other errors. There were in fact three major sins of assumption:

(1) That the population would rise by only 1.25 per cent a year. In fact, it rose by 2 per cent. In a population as large as India's already was, this meant a shortfall of 17 million mouths, and it was estimated that India's population had reached 425 million in 1960–1, instead of the assumed 408 million.

(2) That the encouraging food crops of the first plan would continue. In fact, the monsoon failed in 1957. Grain production dropped by 6.7 million tons and food prices soared by 10 per cent in one year. The planners had assumed India would not need to import more than 6 million tons of food over the five-year period. In reality, the need was of the order of 15 million tons.

(3) That India's foreign exchange requirements ('resources to be raised externally', as the planners airily expressed it) would be about £600 million (in addition to India's own sterling balances, estimated at £150 million) and would easily be forthcoming. The underlying assumption was that the terms of trade would continue to be as favourable to India as they had been in 1954–5. Disaster: they fell back to the 1952–4 level. The trade gap widened alarmingly from £47 million—relatively manageable—to £218 million.

In one respect, however, India was lucky. the Indians, it turned out, had friends—good, generous *capitalist* friends—ready to rescue Pandit Nehru from the consequences of his planners' assumptions. The Eisenhower administration decided to meet India's food import gap from American agricultural surpluses, under the famous Public Law 480, and there would be no charge. In 1958, Britain, West Germany and Japan joined with the US to form the 'aid India club'.

It is perhaps worth quoting the rather grandiose eight basic decisions that were to govern Nehru's and his planners' 'grand strategy in the war against poverty' (as the second five-year plan was termed), in that they typify the woolly thinking inseparable from social democracy:

(1) The second plan must be big—big enough and powerful enough to begin to lift the Indian economy across the 'threshold' to a developed nation.
(2) India will develop first and above all its agriculture and its rural people.
(3) India will develop its industries—but with a careful balancing of large and small industry, of the heavy industries basic to economic growth, and the traditional small and hand industries essential to employment and social stability.
(4) India will increase living standards and consumption at the same time that it builds its industries.
(5) India will take advantage of every possible way of growth consistent with democracy to develop the nation and its people.
(6) India will seek the development of all groups and classes among its people, and of all regions of the nation, so that there may be a growing equality of income and opportunity.
(7) India will at every step of its progress associate the people in the villages and districts with planning and development, so that their initiative, energies and co-operation are awakened and assured, and may serve as the constructive and creative instrument of development itself.
(8) India will, in all its plans and policies, set as its highest single purpose the development of the individual, and his advancement in human freedom.

The second point was merely pious. If it meant anything, it implied that agriculture had a high investment priority. In fact, the second plan alloted only 11 per cent of the budget to agriculture, compared to 50 per cent for industry (the basic Stalinist error from which the socialist regimes of Eastern Europe, including Russia, all suffer). Under the third plan, agriculture was to get 14 per cent: better, but still inadequate, given the size of the problem.

The sixth decision also contained its element of self-righteous piety. The development of 'all groups and classes' sounded admirably egalitarian, and was indeed in line with Nehru's Constitution which forbade discrimination against the *harijans* or 'untouchables'. That this was a provision on paper only could be observed by anybody dropping in at random on any of India's 570,000 villages. Some 80 million Indians remained condemned to clean the latrines and sweep the streets, no matter what the Constitution or the sixth basic decision might say. Similarly, another legacy of Hinduism—the sacred cow—made a nonsense of planning assumptions. Diseased but sacrosanct, some 250 million holy cows competed with the people for India's scarce food resources.

The most important aspect of the basic assumptions, however, was the pursuit of incompatible objectives: centralised planning *and* individual freedom; tolerance of private enterprise and priority of investment for the state; creation of large-scale industries *and* stimulation and protection of the economically unproductive cottage crafts, dear to the heart of Mahatma Gandhi.

Given the performance of private industry, in the face of governmental obstacles, including excessively high taxes, there is little doubt that it could, under more favourable conditions, have gone a long way towards solving India's perennial problem of poverty. But that would not have suited the planners. From the start, Nehru had vested the Planning Commission with virtually limitless economic powers, under the Prime Minister's own chairmanship. Starting from preconceived socialist theory, instead of adapting the economic lessons of history to India's special problems, India's planners made the usual mistakes of *dirigiste* planning. In economic terms, their fundamental error was to give priority to industry over agriculture. In political and philosophical terms, they overlooked the clear correlation between economic and political freedom. True centralised planning can be followed through in practice only when the state conscripts and directs labour, requisitions all materials and smashes any opposition that is bound to manifest itself.

Fortunately, India was saved by its attachment to democracy, not its belief in socialism. Something had to give and (under Nehru, at least) it was usually socialism.

Another thing saved India from the worst the planners could inflict: the capitalist friends I mentioned earlier. In his interesting study, *Leaders* (1982), Richard Nixon wrote:

India needed productivity from the bottom up. Instead on the economic front, it got ideology from the top down, with layer upon layer of flypaper bureaucracy to snare the feet of anything that moved. The United States alone has provided India with more than $9 billion of aid since independence. But this has gone to remedy the results of Socialist failure rather than to build the foundations of a self-sustaining economy. (273)

Burma

By common consent, the Burmese are by nature easy-going and charming. Yet xenophobia is an important element in Burma's history and national character. It is Burma's misfortune that its dictator since 1962 (without counting his previous shortlived rule from 1958), General Ne Win, chose to inflict both a Marxist socialist experiment and official xenophobia upon the many peoples of Burma.

It took Ne Win about twelve years to complete the ruination of Burma which had begun under the inefficient civilian politicians whom he displaced.

In January 1948, Burma became the first of Britain's imperial possessions to gain its independence. With its enormous mineral resources, its rice and its timber, it had every right to expect a flourishing economic future. In their innocence, U Nu and his colleagues told their people that before very long each family could expect a house and a car of their own and no less than £1,500 a year. Alas, by 1974, the average family income at only £200 a year was one of the world's lowest. Burma had absorbed some £500 million in foreign aid, with nothing to show for it, and instead of exporting 3 million tons of rice, as it did in the bad old colonial days, the silos were empty and food riots not uncommon.*

Some of the facts in this chapter are drawn from 'Burma on the Marxist Road to Ruin', an unformative article by Anthony Paul in *Asia Magazine* (Hong Kong) of mid-December 1974, condensed in the British edition of the *Reader's Digest* of January 1976.

Burma's civilian politicians had at least the attraction of inefficiency and an easy-going Buddhist approach to government. Ne Win, half-Chinese and energetic, set Burma on the road to poverty with military efficiency. 'Shared scarcity' was Professor Hugh Tinker's kind euphemism for it. I prefer to call it the 'cult of scarcity'.

Ne Win set out his ideas in a manifesto, *The Burmese Way to Socialism*, which proclaimed two mutually antithetical principles: a commitment to Marxism and the promise of 'a new society for all, economically secure and morally better'. It was the commitment to Marxism that won.

As Anthony Paul records, more than 90 per cent of Burma's commerce and industry was nationalised, creating drastic shortages of all commodities on the home market and—the natural consequence—widespread corruption and a flourishing black market, despite severe penalties. In agriculture, Ne Win went even further than his distant mentors of the Soviet Union, for instance, by 'nationalising' onions, potatoes and beans. All three items promptly disappeared, since the farmers now saw no special reason to produce them. Ne Win's response was typically authoritarian. He decontrolled onions, potatoes and beans; all three rapidly reappeared on the market. He then pounced on the private traders who were handling the reborn items, ordering the Army to seize the more successful firms, and gaoling the successful owners.

As for the xenophobia, Ne Win simply stopped issuing import licences to foreign firms trading in Burma and denied them access to foreign currency. The foreigners had a simple choice: be nationalised or go bust. Most of them left Burma. Tourism was banned, and so were foreign journalists. In its xenophobic vacuum, Burma speeded up its socialist journey into abject poverty.

Tanzania

Julius Nyerere, President of Tanzania (a neologistic amalgam of Tanganyika and Zanzibar), must be granted a natural talent for public relations. A mild-mannered little man, with a soft voice, he rapidly built up a reputation for moderation in Westminster, Whitehall and Fleet Street. In fact, he has shown himself one of the most extreme of the post-independence leaders of Black Africa. The myth, however, prevails. It is distinctly bad form to hint that perhaps, after all, Nyerere is not a 'moderate'.

On a state visit to Britain in 1975, the moderate Mr Nyerere had this to say: 'In one world, as in one state, when I am rich because you are poor, and I am poor because you are rich, the transfer of wealth from rich to poor is a matter of right: it is not an appropriate matter for charity.'

This curious philosophy, which incidentally is economic nonsense, gained astonishingly wide acceptance. For instance, it underlies one of the more absurd documents of recent times, the *Brandt Report* of 1981, in the compilation of which a former British Prime Minister, Edward

Heath, played a leading part. The *Brandt Report* might indeed have been written as a personal favour to Julius Nyerere, and advocated a massive transfer of wealth from the 'rich North' to the 'poor South', of which it could be said, on the basis of simple observation, that it would be a recipe for the rapid further enrichment of an already corrupt official class in the 'developing' countries with nil effect upon the living standards of Third World populations.

I am, however, digressing. The myths of development aid programmes and of Nyerere's alleged moderation were brilliantly exploded in an article by Professor Peter Bauer and John O'Sullivan in the *Spectator* of 25 June 1977. By then, the irreparable damage inflicted on his country by President Nyerere was an accomplished fact. From it I quote:

> Some regimes do not stop at persecuting minorities. Dr Nyerere's government in Tanzania has in the last decade forcibly moved millions of people into collectivised villages and sometimes simply into the bush. Among the methods of encouragement employed are the destruction of existing homes, physical force and barring recalcitrant elements from such social facilities as communal transport, beer shops, ceremonial dances and cattle auctions. The numbers of people subjected to this new life certainly runs into millions. Some estimates are as high as six to eight million (*Washington Post*, 6 May 1975) and even thirteen million (*The Times*, 20 April 1977) out of a total population of fifteen million.

The examples of Burma and Tanzania are admittedly more extreme than those of other socialist experiments, outside the communist countries. But the fact that they are more extreme than some merely proves the points made at the start of Part 2 of this book. The more extreme the socialism, the more extreme the impoverishment. And the more extreme the socialism, the greater the coercion and sufferings of the population. The contradiction between socialism and liberty is total: the more socialism, the less liberty. The social democrat who in the last resort stops short of full socialism because he values democracy understands these points instinctively, although not necessarily willing to concede them intellectually.

10

Welfare Socialism

George Bernard Shaw, in the *Intelligent Woman's Guides* in the 1920s and 1930s, used to delight in reminding his (presumably feminine) audience that all countries, including capitalist ones, practised communism in some aspects of daily life. His examples included roads, railways and postal services. Similarly, one might truly say that all countries, including 'capitalist' ones, practise socialism to some degree or other.

Some degree of socialism may indeed be necessary (although I may be parting company with my distinguished co-author with such a sacrilegious statement). The trouble is to establish how much is needed, where to draw the line. For my part, I favour socialist welfare—for those who need it. The trouble with Welfare socialism as introduced into Great Britain in the post-war Labour government of Clement Attlee is that it is indiscriminate, so that even people who do not need it receive it. I shall not elaborate on the British example, which has been covered by Arthur Seldon in Part 1. But there is no shortage of examples to look at in the Western world. In this chapter, I shall take a selective look at France, Sweden, West Germany, Austria; and the great United States of America.

Two aspects of Western socialism mainly concern us here. The cost and value of Welfare; and the cost of nationalisation, in terms of industry's contribution to a nation's wealth.

France

The example of France is particularly apposite, for the performance in office of the Socialist/Communist government which has governed the

French Republic under President François Mitterrand (and was still in power as these lines were written) is there for all to see. When Mitterrand's coalition came to power in May 1981, France had had about two decades of unprecedented economic growth, rising standards of living and general prosperity. In less than two years, socialism had, in effect, ruined the country. It was an amazing, if negative, achievement.

In 1955, a Swiss journalist called Herbert Luthy wrote a book which caused a sensation in France. Its title, in French, was *La France à L'Heure de son Clocher* (the English translation of which was *'France Keeps its Own Time'*). The France Luthy was writing about was backward in comparison with its neighbours and rivals. Capital equipment was obsolete, investment was inadequate. Any economist bold enough to extrapolate from the data given by Luthy would have concluded that France, in two or three decades, would find itself, let us say, the 'Albania' of Western Europe. Instead, the opposite happened. General de Gaulle came to power in 1958, and gave priority to bringing the expensive Algerian war to a close. He brought in the respected former Prime Minister, Antoine Pinay, as Finance Minister and Pinay dealt with French inflation by the simple expedient of knocking off the last two noughts of France's currency and creating a 'heavy franc'. Recovery and expansion really got under way in 1962. Over the next ten years (1962–72) France's gross national product (GNP) grew from $52,583 million to $273,806 million. In comparison, the British economy, which suffered from creeping socialism, grew from an initially favourable GNP of $62,668 million to no more than $188,543 million. During the whole of the period between 1962 and 1981, France enjoyed the blessings of relative stability under de Gaulle's fifth Republic, under a Constitution tailor-made for de Gaulle. But the real point was that during this entire period, although France itself had a Welfare socialism of its own, the country's finances were under the direction of able conservative technicians, including Giscard d'Estaing, later to become President of the Republic before his defeat at the hands of François Mitterrand. In other words, France had been doing pretty well with *minimal* socialism.

I must be fair to the French Socialists (although fairness is hardly due to the Moscow-line Stalinist French Communist Party which Mitterrand had taken into the coalition because he thought it would be safer to have them inside than outside his government). The coalition took over at a time of deepening international recession. In France itself, unemployment had been mounting, and was past the 2 million mark. French

Socialist doctrine (as is true of socialism everywhere) had an easy prescription for this kind of situation: spend, spend, spend! And nationalise, nationalise, nationalise!

So the government nationalised nearly all the banks and insurance companies, and created some 200,000 phoney jobs in the public sector. Soon, government spending rose uncontrollably. So did unemployment. So did inflation, which was soon double the British rate, and four times the German.

In the non-communist world, there are two standard short-term remedies for this kind of situation: borrow, or print money. The French government did both. It borrowed wildly abroad and kept the printing presses busy. Faced with rising costs and increasing labour militancy, private industry found itself becoming rapidly uncompetitive in the world's markets—exactly as Britain's had during the long years of creeping socialism. The only difference was that the French were moving downhill faster than the British did. Twice, the government devalued the franc. Even that was not enough. The grand climax came in March 1983 with a *third* devaluation and a budget of savage austerity.

The Finance Minister, Jacques Delors, having presided over this man-made ruination, now forced the French taxpayers to pay the price for official follies. Of all the measures announced, the most unpopular was the restriction of the individual allowance for tourists abroad to 2,000 francs (£190 at the new rate) per adult a year, with half that amount for each child. Henceforth, French families were not allowed to use credit cards outside France.

A compulsory savings plan was introduced, equal to 10 per cent of income tax, and a new wealth tax was to be levied by the government on all but the very lowest incomes. In addition, a surcharge equal to 1 per cent in income tax was to be imposed on all incomes. The estimated proceeds of 11,000 million francs were to be used to help balance the social security fund.

From 1 April, all public service charges were increased by 8 per cent. This included gas, electricity, the telephone and railway prices.

Government spending programmes were to be cut by 15,000 million francs, while revenue was to be increased by the introduction of a special tax on oil products. By that time, France's external trade deficit had reached about 100,000 million francs. The new measures, however, were expected to cut domestic consumption by about 65,000 million

francs (£6,200 million) by the end of 1983—equivalent in a full year to about a 2 per cent cut in the gross domestic product.

The Swedish Model

Swedish socialism has certain unique features. For one thing, it has been 'going strong' for a long time: Social Democratic governments were in power continuously for 44 years, until the very left-wing Prime Minister, Olof Palme, fell in 1976. But the mildly 'conservative' government which took over did virtually nothing to counter the trend. By then, Swedish socialism was firmly established by national concensus, and inertia. In 1982, Palme came back to power, and the process resumed.

The most remarkable aspect of Swedish socialism is that, in contrast to most other kinds (ranging from, say, the USSR to the United Kingdom), nationalisation of private companies was, by and large, avoided. The idea was not that the state should grab the means of production; rather, that it should grab the production itself. In other words, the wealth produced by Swedish industry, and the money earned by individuals, was in effect confiscated by the state, in return for the most universal welfare schemes on earth.

The Swedes had other things going for them. One was industrial peace on an almost unrivalled stage (with only Switzerland as a competitor). This went back to the famous Saltsjöbaden agreement of 1938, which repudiated strikes without actually outlawing them. The Swedes, too, enjoyed peace in the more normal sense, meaning the absence of war. A previously warlike nation, they had abandoned war as an instrument of policy, starting in 1815, and living through two world wars without actually getting involved. A sure-fire recipe for prosperity . . .

For about three decades, Swedish socialism appeared to be a going concern. The Swedes had apparently achieved the impossible: free enterprise and socialism were cohabiting, and Sweden had achieved one of the highest standards of living in the world with the widest distribution of social benefits. Despite high spending on defence (to defend their neutrality), they always managed, or so it seemed, to keep afloat. To complete the picture, Sweden had high-grade iron ore in abundance; a flourishing paper and pulp industry served by immense forests; and water power for the asking. And then, in the late 1960s and early 1970s, things began to go wrong. The causes were partly external: in common with other industrial countries, Sweden suffered from the catastrophic rise in oil prices after the Arab—Israeli war of 1973. Shipbuilding was badly hit by falling world demand, and Sweden's excellent iron ore ran into strong competition from countries where it could be more cheaply produced. The main problems, however, were inherent to socialism, even of the Swedish variety. There was probably a theoretical time—let us say, for the sake of argument, around 1965–when the Social Democrats had got the mixture about right, for Sweden's needs, and for the Swedish national character. But the trouble with legislators, especially socialist ones, is that they never know when to stop. The Swedish character itself had been profoundly marked by the decades of socialism. Expecting everything from the state, the worker didn't have much incentive to work, and Sweden developed the highest rate of industrial abstention in the world. Moreover, as is typical of socialist regimes, the bureaucracy kept on expanding. An astute Swedish political observer, Baron Carl von Platen, has described the process admirably in his book, *The Uneasy Truce* (1983) As more and more married women took highly paid jobs, the mobility of Swedish labour was affected: as von Platen put it: 'A husband does not want to move from, say, Stockholm to Malmö if his wife does not also get a good job in the new location.'

But the worst problem of all was the ever-expanding weight of taxes. As taxes increased, incentives for self-betterment decreased. Understandably many Swedes took to 'moonlighting', creating a sizeable black economy. The same phenomenon has occurred in Britain, but in Sweden the disincentives of high taxation were considerably worse. By the time these lines were written, the tax burden in Sweden had risen to 67 per cent of earned income.

The bureaucracy, as measured by the proportion of the country's gross domestic product (GDP) spent by the state, soared from less than 25 per cent in 1950 to more than 60 per cent in 1979. There are only about 8 million Swedes, yet more than 1½ million of them work for the state in one form or another. To put it as simply as possible. Swedish socialism has almost strangled itself with its own bureaucracy.

This brings me back to my third Universal Rule of Socialism: that it is incompatible with freedom. Of course, the Swedes are freer than, say, Soviet or Chinese citizens. But they are far less free than, say, the British, Americans or French. With socialism, the correlation is clear: the more socialism, the less freedom. Some years ago, a basically sympathetic but honest and acute observer of Sweden, Roland Huntford of *The Observer*, wrote a powerful book which said it all in its title: *The New Totalitarians* (New York, 1972). Huntford compares Swedish society with Aldous Huxley's hygienic nightmare of the 1930s, *Brave New World*. It would have been hard to prove that there was repression in Sweden, or that 'human rights' were violated. Certainly, there were neither tortures nor concentration camps. But, as Huntford said, every detail of life was regulated by the bureaucracy, and by increasingly pervasive custom. It was morally unacceptable to the community that one should step out of line. In their 44 years of creeping socialism, the Swedes had realised what Sidney and Beatrice Webb had only dreamed of in the Fabian Society—the 'inevitability of gradualness' had brought universal prosperity and welfare, at a high price in loss of liberty. And then, to complete the picture, the prosperity itself started to drain away.

USA: The Great Society

The word 'socialism' does not readily occur to the European observer of the United States. Yet the original home of the great unbridled capitalists of the early twentieth century—the Fords, the Rockefellers, the Mellons—has by now absorbed a hefty dose of the stuff. It all began with the famous (or notorious) New Deal introduced by President Franklin D. Roosevelt, after his election as the thirty-second President of the United States of America in 1932—at the height of the Great Depression. The New Deal involved a spate of legislation between 1933 and 1936, starting with agriculture and continuing with legislation affecting banking, home financing, gold and silver, relief for the unemployed, securities, labour and social security. Capitalism was to be tamed, and wealth redistributed. The climax came with the Wealth Tax Act of August 1935, which invoked the Federal power of taxation as a weapon against 'unjust concentration of wealth and economic power'. Increased surtaxes on individual yearly incomes of $50,000 and over were introduced.

Roosevelt was a Democrat, and ever since his presidency, welfarism in America has naturally been associated with Democratic administrations. This, however, is misleading. For example, it was the Republican President Dwight D. Eisenhower who launched the much-attacked Department of Health, Education and Welfare (popularly known as HEW) in 1953. True, it was the Democrat, President Lyndon B. Johnson, who legislated for his proposed Great Society in the 1960s, but it was under the Republican Presidents Richard Nixon and Gerald Ford that the expansion of welfare really took off.

In May 1964, President Johnson addressed the graduating class of Michigan University, and declared that 'in your time we have the opportunity to move not only toward the rich society and a powerful society, but upward to the Great Society'. In his *Memoirs*, Richard Nixon was critical of Johnson's concept. The fatal flaw of his Great Society, he wrote, was 'its inclination to establish massive federal programmes' (p 267). In five years, he recalls, Johnson's spending for the poor doubled, from $12.5 billion to $24.6 billion, while federal funds for health and education soared by over $18 billion.

In a powerful, brilliantly written book, *Wealth and Poverty*, the American economist George Gilder lamented the consequences of what he called the 'actuarial state'. Unemployment compensation, he claimed, promotes unemployment. 'Aid for Families with Dependant Children (AFDC) makes more families dependent and fatherless. Disability insurance in all its multiple forms encourages the promotion of small ills into temporary disabilities and partial disabilities into total and permanent ones.' Gilder, whose book (published in 1981) became a kind of Bible for the incoming Republicans under their new President, Ronald Reagan, goes on to record that during the 1970s, forty-four major welfare programmes grew two and a half times as fast as GNP and three times as fast as wages.

I am not sure that I go all the way with Gilder, impressive though his paean of praise for the moral values of capitalism undoubtedly is. He comes close to saying that *all* welfare is bad. I would stop short of so sweeping a condemnation. The problem, I believe, lies—in America as in Sweden and elsewhere—with knowing when to stop. The trouble is that the bureaucracies created by welfare feed on themselves and expand uncontrollably. If the end-result is national impoverishment, nobody benefits in the long term.

That admirable conservative institution, The Heritage Foundation in Washington, DC, has issued some damning reports on the administration of welfare in the United States. In one of them, Jonathon R. Hobbs, under the title 'Welfare Need and Welfare Spending' (13 October 1982) exploded the popular myth that because defence spending was on the increase, welfare spending was necessarily decreasing. Indeed, defence spending *was* increasing: from $187.5 billion in Financial Year 1982, to $221.1 billion in FY 1983. But defence spending was

clearly identifiable as such in its own specific budget. In contrast, welfare spending was disguised in the multiple budgets of 49 major national programmes (up from 44 under President Johnson). If all the items were added together, welfare expenditure for FY 1982 totalled $403.5 billion—more than twice the level of defence spending.

The author is highly critical of the growth of welfare bureaucracy, which had turned into an industry of more than 5 million public and private workers, to service 50 to 60 million recipients. The cost of welfare continued to soar and the nett effect was to perpetuate poverty instead of abolishing it. Indeed, the author made out an excellent case for abolishing 'poverty' while cutting welfare expenditure by up to 75 per cent. (The 'poverty threshold' had been defined by the Social Security Administration in 1964, based upon the amount spent by families of three or more on food.) The study ended with these words: 'When the US is able to focus public assistance on the needs of the poor rather than on the expansionary interests of a government-controlled industry, Americans will save enormous sums of money, eliminate legions of bureaucrats, and better serve the poor.'

Whether this view of welfare was a practical reality, and whether the Reagan administration would seriously set out to slash the welfare industry down to cost-effective proportions, remained to be seen when this book was written.

In America as elsewhere, socialism was exorbitantly expensive.

After the German 'Miracle'

The example of the German Federal Republic (West Germany) is illuminating in ways that are subtly different from our other Western case studies. Everybody has heard of 'the German miracle', which the Germans call their *Wirtschaftswunder*. All that need be said about it here, as a reminder, is that out of the total destruction of World War II, out of all the rubble and the misery, the economist Dr Ludwig Erhard built an amazingly prosperous economy by sweeping away price and wage controls, abolishing rationing and allowing the market to rule. Erhard called his experiment a 'social market economy', to show that he had not forgotten about the legitimate needs of welfare.

Thus under free enterprise and 'capitalism', defeated Germany (or rather the Western two-thirds of it) built the strongest economy in Western

Europe, and (with Japan and the United States) one of the three strongest in the world.

It is often forgotten that this astonishing achievement persisted and improved on its own performance under the Grand Coalition, which was in power in the Federal Republic from 1966 to 1969 when Willy Brandt and his Social Democrats took over.

The grandly called 'Grand Coalition' was so termed because it brought together West Germany's three main parties (or four, if you count the Christian parties separately): the Christian Democrats (CDU) and Christian Social Union (CSU); the Liberals (FDP); and the Social Democrats (SPD). Perhaps the most important aspect of the Grand Coalition was that the Finance portfolio was in the hands of the redoubtable Franz-Josef Strauss, the Bavarian leader of the CSU. I interviewed Strauss at length for *Now!* magazine (15 February 1980). I asked him whether, in the event of his becoming Chancellor in the next elections, he would keep Erhard's 'social market economy' unchanged. His reply is worth quoting in full today, more than three years later:

> I would put it differently. I helped Erhard introduce the social market system as early as June 1948, against the votes of the Communists and Helmut Schmidt's Socialist friends. He was unable to dismantle it, but he inherited it from us.
>
> In fact, on his own past and even recent record, Mr Schmidt is an opponent of the system. The SPD wanted centralised economic planning and advocated the so-called 'Deutschland Plan'. If they had succeeded, we would have had a confederation with the East German Communists, with poverty and dependence on Moscow as the inevitable consequences.
>
> Over the past ten years, the State sector of the economy has grown from 37 per cent to 47 per cent. During our 20 years in government (with myself as Finance Minister in Chancellor Kiesinger's Grand Coalition), our public debt totalled 14 billion DM for the whole period. During *each* of Helmut Schmidt's year in power, the public debt grew by more than 150 per cent of our accumulated total. Today, the debt is gigantic. I would not change the social market system, therefore: I would restore it to full efficiency.

Unfortunately, Strauss lost the elections in the spring of 1980. Schmidt and his Liberal friends came back. And the downward slide continued.

It would be unfair, perhaps to rely entirely on the obviously interested verdict of Franz-Josef Strauss upon his rival Schmidt's socialist experiment. In fact, the same picture, in far greater detail, is painted in the OECD's Economic Survey on *Germany* for 1981–2 (published in June 1982, and the latest available when these lines were written). Here are some direct quotations (with key phrases italicised):

> At the end of 1981, the public debt reached DM 545 billion, or 35 per cent of GNP . . . the authorities satisfied their financial requirements mainly in the form of loans against borrowing notes . . .
>
> Over the last twenty years the public sector has absorbed a *markedly increased share of total national output* and has been responsible for the redistribution of a greatly increased proportion of total national income . . .
>
> As far as the redistribution of income is concerned, the rapid growth of social security benefits and grants has added considerably to the growth of total household income *but has been outweighed by increases in direct taxes and social security contributions* with the overall result that transfers from the household to the government sector now represent about 18½ per cent of household disposable incomes, compared with just over 9 per cent at the beginning of the 1960s. Enterprises have been less affected by increases in direct taxes but have had to adjust to a large rise in employers' social security contributions which, as a proportion of operating surplus, have doubled from 15 per cent in 1960 to 30 per cent in 1980 (pp. 34–35).

In other words, the average family was drawing more in social security benefits than it used to do, but was paying out proportionately more than it got for the privilege. Welfare socialism, even of the comparatively mild West German variety, comes expensive. It is fair to ask, however, why the government should be charging the public more than it delivers in terms of education and health services (the main items involved). The OECD Survey gives part of the answer in my next quotation:

> Although government has increased its value share of final expenditure on goods and services, a large part of this increase is attributable to *the faster rise in the cost of providing public rather than private goods and services,* itself a function of *the higher wage content of government activity . . . and its lower growth in productivity.* (p. 37; emphasis added.)

To be more precise, although the OECD Survey did not make the point, the bureaucracy grows faster than the socialist benefits provided. In fact, between 1969 and 1980 the number of citizens whose livelihood in one way or another depended on the state soared from 2.9 million to

4.4 million. To be honest, these figures are cited in a factual survey prepared by *Verlag Information für die Wirtschaft* ('Information of the Economy' Publishers) in Bonn for the then main opposition party, the Christian Democratic Union (CDU), now, of course, in power with its Bavarian counterpart the Christian Social Union (CSU). But the figures correspond with other relevant statistics in the OECD Survey, which, for instance, records that between 1960 and 1980 government expenditure (expressed as a percentage of Gross Domestic Product) rose from 32 to 47 per cent. Even the UK's government expenditure, during the same period, rose 'only' to 45.5 per cent (from 32.6).

While government expenditure rose, so did unemployment. From its lowest point in 1965, when only 147,000 or 0.7 per cent of the labour force were out of work, unemployment rose inexorably under Social Democratic rule, reaching an estimated 2,350,000 or 9.5 per cent in 1983. I do not want to 'labour' this point, however, in the context of an argument over the disadvantages of socialism. In the early 1980s, the industrialised world as a whole was in the grip of deep recession. In Britain, where with Mrs Thatcher's Tory government in power, unemployment soared to more than 3.3 million. It would be wrong, therefore, to attribute Germany's unemployment purely to the effect of socialism in power— even if, as I believe, the underlying causes of Britain's bad performance certainly included the decades of trade union pressure for wage increases unsupported by higher productivity.

Nor am I, as may appear, against rising social welfare. Where welfare socialism in advanced countries has gone off the rails, is in the insistence upon equal benefits for all, regardless of need. This kind of 'equality' is a bottomless financial pit. Selective benefits for the really needy—the old, the truly sick, the handicapped—could indeed be much higher than they are, in West Germany and elsewhere. And higher benefits on a selective basis could well be met without incurring massive, or indeed any budgetary deficits. Unless a government can meet the bills, without running up state expenditures and public debt, welfare is a bad bargain for the voters. The Federal Republic is by no means the worst example of welfare socialism in the West, but the economic distortion caused by egalitarian doctrinalism is characteristic.

An acute observer of the German (and international) economic scene, Dr Herbert Schmidt (a surviving pupil of the great Erhard) recorded further facts and figures in *International Management into the 1990s*.* In a table on p. 17, Dr Schmidt recorded that the German public debt had risen by only 14 per cent from 1960 to 1970, but by 276 per cent from 1970 to 1980. As a percentage of GNP, the public debt stood at 17.2 per cent in 1960, at 18.5 per cent in 1970 and at 31 per cent ten years later. In 1980 *Federal debts alone for the first time exceeded the Federal budget.*

To this dangerous trend should be added the extraordinary readiness of the private banks in the Federal Republic to collect bad debts in the form of constantly 'rescheduled' loans to the Soviet bloc countries, especially Poland. As I have pointed out elsewhere, the West German banks are not alone in this folly, but they have indulged in it to an even greater extent than other banking systems.

The collapse of the coalition led by Helmut Schmidt and his Social Democrats in the autumn of 1982 and the subsequent sweeping victory of the Christian parties in the general elections of March 1983 may have rescued the Federal Republic from the impending consequences of socialism on the loose. It is too early to declare how successful the Christian Democrats and the Christian Social Union will be in dealing with the inherited mess.

'Partnership' in Austria

Whenever the debate about socialism starts up, somebody is sure to raise a hand and ask: 'What about Austria, then? Thirteen years of socialism, and the Austrians are doing very nicely, thank you.' Or words to that effect.

Let us, then, look at the Austrian example. The short answer to the kind of remark I have just quoted is that the Socialists were in power in Austria for thirteen years until Chancellor Bruno Kreisky fell in the 1983 elections, but the Austrian economic system could hardly be described as 'socialist'. Alternatively, it was a rather peculiar, indeed unique, form of socialism.

The OECD Economic Survey of *Austria*, 1982, gives a concise description of the Austrian system. After World War II, the Austrian Parliament decided *unanimously* to nationalise all the major sectors of the economy: the largest banks, the electricity companies and most of the steel, mining, engineering and chemical industries. By the 1980s, the public sector employed about 30 per cent of the work force. Taking the

*Edited by L.L. Waters for Indiana University; papers presented at an international conference, 27 September–1 October 1981.

fifty largest enterprises, however, the state-owned sector accounted for more than two-thirds of the total.

These facts alone might seem to qualify Austria for inclusion among the socialist states, at least by Western criteria. When it comes to *control* over the economy, however, the state turns out to be pretty feeble. It is not the government that determines economic policy, still less the elected Parliament. All economic policy decisions of importance are taken by the 'Social Partnership'—in practice, by a body known as the *Paritätische* Kommission ('Parity Commission'), a *privately* constituted body comprising equal representation of the trade unions, the employers' associations and the farmers' unions. The economic ministers do have a say, but strictly as junior partners.

To quote the OECD Survey: 'After the experience of civil war, political persecution and foreign occupation, political parties and social groups decided to bury their ideological differences and co-operate on a basis of equality, creating a political system that can be characterised as a parliamentary democracy with important *corporative* elements.' (p. 23; my emphasis).

Oh dear! Wasn't it Mussolini who based his fascist state on the corporative principle? Does that mean Austria has a form of fascism? Let us not play with emotive words. The notion of 'corporations' representing economic and social interests was probably the one constructive idea in Mussolini's fascism. It may hurt some readers to say so, but the nearest equivalent to Austria's Parity Commission in recent European history was General Franco's 'vertical' trade unions (known as *sindicatos*), in which the employers as well as the workers were represented. The main difference—an important one—was that the Spanish *sindicatos* were in the last resort dominated by Franco's political organisation, known as the Movement, whereas the Austrian Parity Commission virtually excludes the government from decision-making.

In a perceptive article in *The Journal of Economic Affairs*, London, of January 1982, the Austrian economist Professor Erich Streissler, illustrated the point about governmental impotence in these words: ' . . . to the amusement of the nation, he [Kreisky] has now found twice that he cannot even get rid of his Minister of Finance, Androsch, if the trade unions do not agree.'

This may seem like the kind of socialism Britain's still inordinately powerful unions like, but appearances are deceptive. Unlike Britain's trade unions, the Austrian ones practise wage restraint to an almost unbelievable degree. Professor Streissler records that in 1979 and 1980, at a time when the economy grew by 9 per cent, the President of the trade union federation, Anton Benya, decreed practically constant wages, and 'without creating unrest!'.

Let Streissler give his verdict: 'The whole system can be called 'socialist' only by a heroic stretch of political imagination.'

So, yes, the Austrians did pretty well under a government of Socialists. But they were *not* living under a socialist system. My Universal Rules of socialism therefore remain unaffected by the Austrian example.

CONCLUSION

To borrow from Euclid: *quod erat demonstrandum.*

Index

Africa, 106
   socialism in, 4, 31
   Cuban forces in, 100
Albania, socialism in, 82
Allais, Professor Maurice, 7
Andropov, Yuri, 62
Attlee, Clement, 114
Australasia, 3
Austria, 127–9
   socialism in, 5, 29, 127

Babeuf, François, 8
Bakunin, Mikhail Alexandrovitch, 54
Barone, Enrico, 59
Basnett, David, 52
Batista, Fulgencio, 101
Bauer, Professor Peter, 113
Benn, Tony, 52
Benya, Anton, 129
Berlin, Soviet removal of capital
   equipment from, 87
   Wall, 89
Bevan, Aneurin, 27
Blanc, Louis, 54
Böhm-Bawerk, Eugen von, 47
Bojanic, Milenko, 84
Bolsheviks, 72
   65th Anniversary of Revolution
   (1982), 80

Brandt, Willy, 62
   – Heath Commission, 62
   Brandt Report (1981), 112
Britain, capitalism in, 29
   limited 'democratic' socialism in, 13
British Labour Party, 52
British Parliament, 33
Brezhnev, Leonid, 79
   détente, 80
Brus, Professor Wlodzimierz, 47, 61
Bukovsky, Vladimir, 47
Bulgaria, socialism in, 29
Burma, 111–12
   socialism in, 111

Canada, 32
Castro, Fidel, 100
   speech to Cuban National
   Assembly (1979), 101
Ceausescu, Nicolae, 83
Chapple, Frank, 52
Chinese People's Republic, 94–8
   Cultural Revolution (1966), 97
Cohn, Professor Norman, 55
Comecon, 82
Council for Mutual Economic Aid,
   see Comecon
Conquest, Robert, 77

131

Cuba, 94, 100–3
Czechoslovakia, 90–92
'Prague Spring', 91
socialism in, 91

Delors, Jacques, 116
d'Estang, Giscard, 115
de Gaulle, General, 115
Dickinson, H. D., 49
Djilas, Milovan, 77
Dobb, Maurice, 49
Dragosavac, Dusan, 84
Dubcek, Alexander, 91
Durbin, Evan, 49

Eastern Europe, 82–93
Soviet forces' intervention in, 82
East Germany, 87–90
socialism in, 29, 87
Eisenhower Administration, 108, 120
Eisenhower, Dwight D., 120
Engels, Friedrich, 72
Communist Manifesto (1848), 72
see also Karl Marx
Erhard, Dr Ludwig, 89
Eurocommunism, 6

Fabian Society, 120
see also Webb, Sidney and Beatrice
Federal Republic of Germany, Grand Coalition in, 124
First Indo-China War, 94
Fletcher, Raymond, 49
Foot, Michael, socialism of, 7
wartime economic system, 14–16
France, 114–18
socialism in, 62
Franco, 128

General Agreement on Tariffs and Trade (GATT), 84
Germany, National Socialism in, 13
socialism in, 88
Ghana, socialism in, 106
Gheorghiu-Dej, Gheorghe, 85
Gierek, Edward, 92
Gilder, George, 121
Gill, Ken, 52
Gomulka, Wladyslaw, 91
Greece, socialism in, 62
Guinea, 106

Hattersley, Roy, socialism of, 20, 52
Hayek, F. A. von, 59–60
Healey, Denis, 52
Heath, Edward, 112,
Brandt Report (1981), 112
Heffer, Eric, socialism of, 20, 61
Hitler, Adolf, 56
Hobbs, Jonathan R., 121
Hobsbawn, Eric, 11
political socialism of, 61
Ho Chi Minh City (Saigon), 94
Holland, Stuart, 56
Honecker, Erich, 62
Hong Kong, 98
Houphouet-Boigny, Felix, 106
Hume, David, 'siege economy' of, 14
Hungary, socialism in, 58
Huntford, Roland, 71, 119
Husak, Gustav, 91
Huxley, Aldous, 120

India, 106–12
Aid India Club, 109
Community Development Programme in, 107
Gandhi, Mahatma, 110
Gandhi, Mrs Indira, 107

Nehru, Jawaharlal, 106
Nehru, Pandit, 108
  socialism in, 107
Indonesia, socialism in, 106
Italy, fascist socialism in, 13
International Monetary Fund
  (IMF), 87
Ivory Coast, 106

Jaruzelski, J., 62
Johnson, Lyndon, 121

Kadar, Janos, 91
Kautsky, Karl, 50, 59
Keito, Modibo, 106
Kellner, Peter, 51–2
KGB, 47
Khrushchev, Nikita, 73
Kim Il Sung, 86
Kinnock, Neil, 7
  socialism of, 20, 52
Kolakowski, Leszek, 53, 56, 61
Korea, North, 69, 98
  South, 98
Kornai, J., 61
Kosygin, Andrei, 79
Kreisky, Bruno, 127

Labour National Executive
  Committee, 63
Lange, Oskar, 59
Lasky, Melvin, 55
League of Communists, 84
Le Duan, 99
Lenin, P. U., 51
  New Economic Policy (NEP),
  74
Lerner, Max, 49
Liberman, Professor Yevsei, 79
Lincoln, Abraham, 33
Lippmann, Walter, 17
Liska, Tibor, 27
Liu Shao-ch'i, 97

Luard, Evan, 53
Luthy, Herbert, 115
Luxemberg, Rosa, 59

Malenkov, Georgi, 78
Mali, 106
Mao Tse-tung, 67
  'Great Helmsman', 95
  'Great Leap Forward' (1958), 95
  'Great Proletarian Revolution'
  (1966), 97
  street committees, 71
Marx, Karl, 3
  Communist Manifesto (1848),
  72
  prophecy of revolution, 77
  'to each according to his needs',
  54
  see also Friedrich Engels
Miliband, Ralph, 61
Mitterand, François, 114
Morgenthau, Henry J., 87
Mussolini, Benito, 128

National Health Service in Britain,
  40
Ne Win, 111
Netherlands, 32
Nixon, Richard, 110
Nkrumah, Kwame, 106
North America, 3
North Korea, socialism in, 69
Nove, Professor Alec, 11, 50
Nyerere, Julius, 106
  links with England, 112

OECD, 39
OPEC, oil crisis (1973–4), 92
  price rises in, 92
O'Sullivan, John, 113
Owen, David, 7

Palme, Olof, 71, 118,
Parity Commission in Austria, 128
Paul, Anthony, 112
Pinay, Antoine, 115
Pitt, William, 21
Poland, 91–2
    socialism in, 58
    workers' riots in, 91–2
Powell, Enoch, 20
Poznan, workers' riots (June
    1956), 91

Reagan, Ronald, 70
Robbins, Lord, 17
Romania, 85–7
    socialism in, 83, 92
Roosevelt, Franklin D., 120

Saint-Simon, Comte de
    (1760–1825), 8
Scandinavia, 32
Schmidt, Dr Herbert, 126
Second World War, 13
Senegal, 106
Senghor, Leopold, 106
Shaw, George Bernard, 114
Shcharansky, Anatoly, 47
Shinwell, Emanuel, 11
Shore, Peter, socialism of, 20, 52
Short, Philip, 46
Sik, Ota, 61
Simis, Konstantin, 38, 46, 47
Singapore, 106
Sirc, Dr Ljubo, 26
Smith, Hedrick, 40, 43
'Socialist Commonwealth', 70
Solidarity (Polish independent
    trade union), 92
Soper, Lord, 5
South America, 31
South Korea, 98
Soviet Communist Party (CPSU),
    72

Spain, socialism in, 62
Stalin, J. V., 52
    First Five-Year Plan, 75
    see also Trotsky
Strachey, John, 56
Strauss, Franz-Josef, 124
Streissler, Professor Erich, 128
Sukarno, Ahmed, 106
Sweden, 5
    Saltsjobaden agreement (1938),
        118
    socialism in, 5, 29, 62
Switzerland, capitalism in, 29

Taiwan, Nationalist regime in, 98
Tanzania, socialism in, 112
Taylor, Charles, 54
Teng, Hsiao-ping, 97–98
Thatcher, Margaret, 70
Third World, socialism in, 104–13
Thompson, E. P., 61
Tinker, Professor Hugh, 111
Titmuss, Richard, 14
Tito (Josip Broz), 83
Toure, Sekou, 106
Townsend, Professor Peter, 30
Trotsky, Leon, 51
    power struggle with Stalin, 75

Universal Rules of Socialism, 67
U Nu, 106
USA, 120–23
    limited 'democratic' socialism in,
        13
USSR, 72–81
    'Reluctant Soviet Market
        Economy', 47

Varley, Eric, 32, 52
Verdet, Ilie, 87
Vietnam, 69
    French in, 100

invasion of Kampuchea
(Cambodia), 99
von Mises, Ludwig, 49
Von Platen, Baron Carl, 119

war economy, 14
Webb, Sidney and Beatrice, 120
see also Fabian Society
Welfare socialism, 114–29
West Germany, 'Economic
Miracle' in, 89

socialism in, 88
Wieser, Friedrich, 53

Yugoslavia, 26, 83–5
joins General Agreement on
Tariffs and Trade (GATT)
(1966), 84
socialism in, 26
communism in, 83
Young, Michael (Lord), social
democracy of, 7, 53